Vintage

Jewelry

FOR
INVESTMENT
AND CASUAL WEAR

KAREN L. EDEEN

COLLECTOR BOOKS

A Division of Schroeder Publishing Co., Inc.

The current values in this book should be used only as a guide. They are not intended to set prices, which vary from one section of the country to another. Auction prices as well as dealer prices vary greatly and are affected by condition as well as demand. Neither the authors nor the publisher assumes responsibility for any losses that might be incurred as a result of consulting this guide.

On the cover, clockwise from top: Zuni carved fetish necklace, $500.00 – 600.00 (p.63). Mexican cabochon onyx and silver bracelet, $175.00 – 250.00 (p.154). Matisse/Renoir enameled copper maple leaf pins. Each pin has matching earrings. Pins, $85.00 – 125.00 each. Earrings $45.00 – 75.00 pair (p.79). Mexican sterling bracelet, $150.00 – 200.00 (p.154). Coro parure, (bracelet not shown here) celdadon-colored chaton and prong-set stones, $225.00 – 265.00 (p.25). Mexican carved head onyx and sterling bracelet, $150.00 – 250.00 (p.154).

Cover design by Beth Summers
Book design by Beth Ray

Searching For A Publisher?

We are always looking for people knowledgeable within their fields. If you feel that there is a real need for a book on your collectible subject and have a large comprehensive collection, contact Collector Books.

COLLECTOR BOOKS
P.O. Box 3009
Paducah, Kentucky 42002-3009
www.collectorbooks.com

Copyright © 2002 by Karen Edeen

Contents

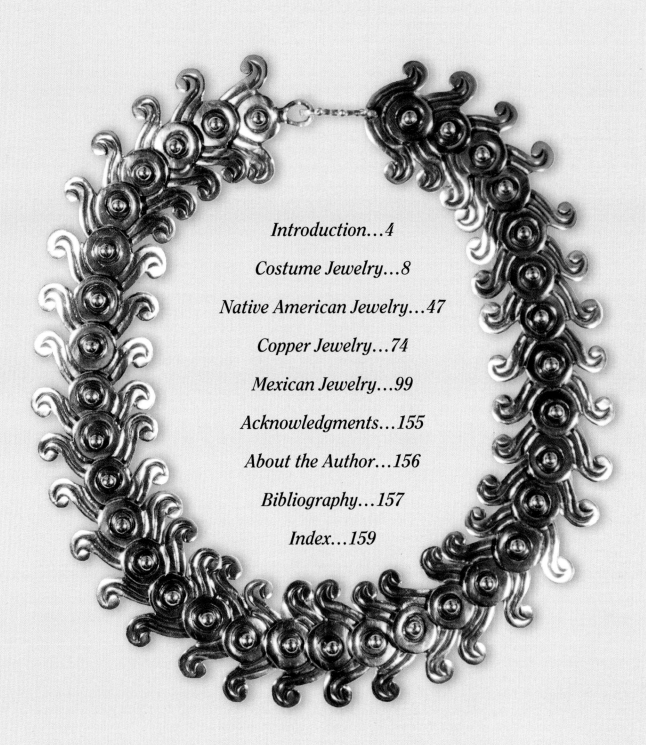

Introduction

The earliest humans were embellishing themselves with natural objects such as shells, animal teeth, feathers and fish vertebrae by the Paleolithic period (25,000 – 12,000 B.C.); the enhancement of the human body with ornaments has been practiced ever since. Man's preoccupation with the simple act of decorating himself with diverse materials has helped generate a spate of assumptions about the course of human history. Examination of jewelry and other artful objects encountered in primordial burial sites has enabled the identification and dating of major prehistoric eras. Jewelry has imparted such illuminating information as remote civilizations' cultural compositions, artistic achievements, trade and migratory routes, and even theories of worship. In addition to contributing clarity to unchronicled times, jewelry has also established facts specific to each occupant found in an ancient grave. Personal artifacts discovered entombed with the deceased indicated their political or social status. Jewels have been venerated as adornment, a symbol of power, and an indicator of material wealth for thousands of years in every culture. The importance of jewelry was demonstrated by the primitive propensity toward burying bodies with their most prized possessions.

There are many examples of the primeval practice of interring valuables with the deceased. Two children of the Ice Age were uncovered in Sungir, Russia, with more than 3,000 ivory beads scattered around their skeletons. The bones of a Bronze Age man were discovered in Bohemia buried with garnet beads, which had been drilled for use in a necklace, strewn near him. Over three thousand years ago, Tutankhamun's sumptuous sarcophagus was carefully packed with the pharaoh's collection of bejeweled collars, bracelets, and breastplates. A Scythian (a nomadic group in the Ukraine who put almost all their personal wealth into portable jewelry — it's been told that seeing Scythian females striding around camp at sunset arrayed in their gold headpieces, dangling earrings, necklaces, and belts was a dazzling sight indeed) male from around 700 B.C. was disinterred with his treasure of a gold earring as well as various gold beads, buttons, and plaques which had been sewn onto his clothing. Ancient Hopewell Indian burial mounds (c. 100 B.C. – A.D. 350) in what is now called Ohio — were found to contain heaps of freshwater pearl necklaces. Under a pyramid in Palenque, Mexican archaeologists uncovered a stone coffin containing the corpse of Lord Shield Pacal (king from A.D. 615 – 683) which was festooned with jade rings on every finger, pounds of jade necklaces and pendants on the chest, and a jade mosaic mask, complete with eyes of obsidian and shell, on the face. In fact, entombing the dead with their jewels was a universally accepted protocol until 800 A.D. when Charlemagne forbade the practice in Europe because it removed too much wealth from circulation.

Gems of great material worth have always been one of the most international and timeless forms of currency. They were often employed throughout history by world leaders to finance the functioning of their nations both in times of peace and times of conflict. Jewels were pledged in order to build roads, create water systems, and fund explorations. Queen Isabella of Castille, Spain, paid for Christopher Columbus' first expedition to America by selling some of her family's jewelry (a portion of these historical pieces was purchased from Tiffany's in the 1890s by the wife of California's Leland Stanford, millionaire builder of railroads). On occasion, both the great and the common have relied upon their jewelry to ensure fealty or to subsidize wars. Roman pearls "were assigned such tremendous value that entire military campaigns could be financed by the sale of a single pearl." (Joyce & Addison, pg. 85.) Norse rulers of the perpetually pillaging Vikings presented local officials with valuables such as "arm rings" to guarantee their allegiance and as a payment of tribute during the turbulent ninth century. Henry III of France wore the fifty-carat Sancy diamond as a decoration on his omnipresent cap (which hid premature baldness), but in 1589 the gem had to be pawned to hire twelve thousand Swiss mercenaries to fight a battle for France. And who could forget the dance scene in "Gone With The Wind" where a donation of jewelry from the ladies was taken up to help finance the faltering Confederate army during the Civil War. Melanie quietly sacrificed her wedding ring ("it will help Ashley more this way than on my finger"), followed by Scarlett who joyfully tossed her ring in with the rest.

Jewels have also long functioned as security against hard times for both women and men. Jung Chang, in the book *Wild Swans,* describes her grandmother's life as a concubine to a great Chinese warlord in the late 1700s. She writes: "On his departure, as on his arrival, he showered jewels on my grandmother — gold, silver, jade, pearls, and emeralds. Like many men of his kind, he believed this was the way to a woman's heart. For women like my grandmother, jewelry was their only insurance." After abandonment by a warlord for a new concubine, these women would be forced to sell their jewelry to support themselves in old age. Men too had their own kind of treasured adornments. Throughout history, men have sported variously valued buttons, buckles, breastplates, sword hilts, rings, and later, watches and cufflinks. These served as testaments to their status and when needed, a guarantee against hardship. The average male's attire was primarily pragmatic but even pirates such as Captain

Kidd wore silver and gold buttons. "So did every pirate. It was a means of combining utility with value on one's own person. A man with a suit embellished with twenty gold and sixty silver buttons was never broke." ("A Mystery in Miniature," *Smithsonian*, Jan. 2000, pgs. 20-21.)

In desperate circumstances, jewelry has long been regarded as one of the most valuable of personal possessions. Excruciating evidence of this truth can be seen in the book, *Nicholas and Alexandra* by Robert Massie, who movingly relates the last days of the imprisoned Russian Romanov Tsar and his family. About the execution which occurred in 1917 he writes: "Behind their mother stood the four girls and Dr. Botkin, the valet Trupp, the cook Kharitonov, and Demidova, the Empress's parlor maid. Demidova carried two pillows, one of which she placed in the chair behind the Empress' back. The other pillow she clutched tightly. Inside, sewed deep into the feathers, was a box containing a collection of the Imperial jewels." Massie goes on to write about the disposing of the bodies. "As the ax blades cut into the clothing, many of the jewels sewed inside were crushed and the fragments spilled out into the high grass or were ground in the mud. . . Most of the personal jewelry taken by the Empress and her daughters to Tobolsk was discovered during the destruction of their bodies." After the execution, part of Alexandra's jewels eventually made their way to Nicholas' mother, who had luckily escaped to Denmark before the revolution. She lived there in a safe country for the remainder of her life off the proceeds from the sale (to a jewelry in New York City — valuable stones have amazingly comparable values in the capitals of the world) of a single stone each year.

Though the previous anecdotes refer to precious gems of considerable intrinsic worth, jewelry offers another trove of treasures beyond strings of pearls and costly stones. Jewelry can be of value whether it is made of costly constituents or not. You do not need gold and genuine gems to have investment caliber jewels. Pieces exist which are constructed of quality materials and timeless design and are unequivocal works of art. As with a Van Gogh painting or the original draft of Abraham Lincoln's Gettysburg Address, value comes from a unique expression of genius which transcends time, and not simply from the intrinsic worth of the respective mediums of canvas and paint, paper and graphite. Similarly, most people feel that there is more value to the symphonies of Mozart than merely sounds to the ear. Popular consensus confers merit to his music and concedes that it is a gift to humanity. So what constitutes "intrinsic" value? A rarity factor? A general consensus? An example of genius? A quality of extreme beauty? A phenomenon of nature? These rhetorical questions infer that the meaning of "intrinsic worth" resides in the mind of the contemplator and is somewhat open to interpretation. Even many of the Spaniards who conquered sixteenth century Mexico and subsequently melted down the gold products of famed Mixtec jewelers (to be made into bars and shipped to Spain) recognized the artistry that they were destroying. Spanish chronicler Peter Martyr wrote, "I do not marvel at gold, but I am astonished to see workmanship excel substance." For our purposes, jewelry which required handcrafted workmanship, entailed tedious time-consuming techniques, and is composed of quality long-lasting materials is valuable and can be considered a worthy candidate for investment.

Webster's dictionary defines "investment" as follows: "to put money into business, real estate, stocks, bonds, etc. for the purpose of obtaining an income or profit." There is no established way to compare jewelry's performance against traditional investment alternatives, but as with any other carefully chosen investment, jewelry can increase your net worth. If you want to accumulate wealth, you need to invest your money in assets that appreciate. You can consume your money on high status items such as designer clothes, the latest cars, or exotic vacations but for ordinary folk, the key to achieving financial security requires frugality in nonessential spending. You want to use limited funds to their maximum potential and, as every investment guide counsels, those funds should be allocated into several different types of investments. Naturally, stocks, bonds, money markets, and real estate constitute the backbone of your investment strategy. But you might consider antique and collectible jewelry as a couple of rib bones around your heart which contribute strength to your financial structure by diversifying your portfolio. Certain jewelry, based on its intrinsic worth, the beauty of its design, or the reputation of its maker, has historically proven itself to be an investment of a most stable and dependable kind.

There are some types of financial transactions which are termed "utility" by economists. This type refers to an investment which is not only measured in monetary terms but also involves the use of the asset. A home exemplifies a venture with both monetary value (generally appreciating in market price over time) and utilitarian value (providing shelter). Jewelry is another case in point of this duality. Since time immemorial almost every human being has owned some piece of jewelry, which implies both its inherent worth and desirability as one of the most used of possessions. Roman senator Seneca (c. 3 B.C. – A.D. c. 65), a kind of dour old soul, reportedly mocked the women of his time in their passion for pearls, decrying, "Simply one for each ear? No! The lobes of our ladies have attained a special capacity for supporting a great number. . . they wear the value of an inheritance in each ear." In long-established tradition in old Mexico, females wore paraphernalia made to display the largest amount of gold coins and ornaments that its owner could accumulate. They especially enjoyed displaying the family's finery at festive dances where jewels were "fastened to the dresses so that every coin shows, the girls' fingers are covered with wide gold rings. . . for they are exhibiting their dowries." And in India, the family fortune was and often still is worn as a necklace around a woman's neck or in the form of bracelets, ear-rings, or rings. As Harrice Miller in *Costume Jewelry* contends, "Costume jewelry has two functions: adornment and investment. Today's rising prices verify that it's not a casual purchase."

As opposed to purchasing antique jewelry, when you buy new jewels from a chain or department store, you are paying retail price, which is the highest price that you can pay. The cost of operating a store includes rent, employee salaries, advertising, taxes, and security systems which are all costs of operating a business. These costs can account for 65% of retail price and are passed along to the consumer in order for the store to make a profit. Even television shopping networks need to pay high overhead costs such as cable network, employees to handle transactions, show production, and administrative costs. It may be worth it to you to pay these costs because you feel that you have the assurance of authenticity and the backing of the network's or store's reputation, but even so, new jewelry depreciates in value because of these operation costs. Buying antique jewels is analogous to buying a used car. A few months after buying a new car, it is now a used car and its value has already started to depreciate. You've lost thousands of dollars just driving off the lot. But by buying a two- or three-year-old car in good condition, its "cash liquidity value" is retained. You could turn around and sell the car for what you paid for it, if you chose wisely. Well bought is half sold. The same princi-ple applies to antique jewelry. The depreciation has already taken place, and now it is a stable or appreciating asset.

Current appreciation, combined with timeless fascination with ornamentation, establishes fine vintage jewel-ry as a viable investment. Maximum cash liquidity in vintage jewelry is possible if you've educated yourself and bought primarily signed jewelry in excellent condition. Appraise your potential purchase and make an objective measure of market price by perusing collectible jewelry books, shopping around, and going to exhibitions. Stay with inexpensive pieces until you are educated about what stamps to search out and develop a discriminating eye for superior design. Seeing the mark of certain manufacturers on jewelry gives assurance of commitment to a high quality product. Most jewelry was marked by the mid 1930s. Buy quality rather than quantity. Use a loupe (a good one is a Rubin and Son Triplet 10 x 20.5mm Antwerp loupe which can be purchased at a jewelry supply store) to carefully examine your considered piece. Look for good condition, no missing parts, no obvious repairs, original packaging if possible, an entire set or parure (three or more of a matched group), and construction of fine caliber materials. Evaluate the complexity of the jewel. Did it require an extended amount of time, endeavor, and talent to create? Prodigious effort is likely to produce a superior product. Aesthetic quality, the eye-appeal of its design, is essential both for your enjoyment and its investment value.

Today's interest in antique and recent vintage fashion has naturally progressed to a passion for period jewelry. A variety of antique and collectible costume, Native American, copper, and Mexican jewelry, which for our purpos-es dates from the 1920s through the 1970s, offers innumerable choices for almost every taste. They are classics which accent current fashion while transcending superficial and transient clothing trends. These quality types of jewelry can be a boon to your spirit and spice up the "glad rags" you wear in your everyday life. Try slipping a few Renoir copper bangles on your wrist or bedeck your shoulder with a whimsical Weiss butterfly. You could revel in a Mexican maestro's masterpiece or in a Native American article, many of which were believed to have conferred vital powers to their owners. We Americans have the highest retail square footage per capita combined with the most consumer debt than anywhere else in the world. Why not consider reducing your debt by scrimping on depreciating items like clothing which can swiftly become passé and splurge on appreciating assets which add to your financial security? The *Collectors Compass* (a book endorsed by the International Society of Appraisers, the leading association of professionally educated and certified personal property appraisers, auctioneers, and dealers) declares, "In general, prices for antique jewelry have increased 20% – 30% each year in the 1990s."

Of course we all need some clothes, so here are some considerations. Most of our lives are complex, hectic, and multifaceted. One way to help reduce stress is to simplify our wardrobes to the basic and the classic. Maximize the potential of your apparel by developing a formula which minimizes time-wasting deliberations and will work for many occasions. Try using the formula components of uncomplicated (solid shade and neutral color) clothes and investment jewels. A summery white outfit is an achromatic setting that can be accented with a colorful cotton sweater tied at the hips and worn with virtually any style of jewelry. Gray garments look great with sterling silver, which brings out and brightens skin tones. Celadon green, cream, pale blue or really any color can serve as a background for your art. Plain black or brown ensembles can be worn day and night, in every season, and when accessorized appropriately, can take you anywhere. Other accoutrements such as sweaters, shawls, and bags can pick up a hue or spark a contrast with your choice of jewels. You could minimize shopping time by ordering through a catalog or over the Internet.

If you really want to minimize spending money on clothing, try thrift shops. Incredible bargains can be found in select thrift shops. Look for those located near posh (The word "posh" originated in the early twentieth century when rich Americans booked trips on luxury ocean liners. They would demand to travel "Port-side Over" to Europe and then after months of vacationing, they would return "Starboard Home.") areas where donations are likely to be upscale. One example of this is a Sacramento Hospice Thrift shop, which is located just blocks away from the neighborhood where Ronald Reagan lived when he was governor of California. A chain of thrift shops found throughout the nation is the Discovery shops of the American Cancer Society. They offer above-average quality and sometimes, absolutely new merchandise at very affordable prices. Caliber brands such as Versace, Donna Karan, Brooks Brothers, Anne Klein, Banana Republic, Escada, Gucci, Nordstrom, Saks Fifth Avenue, Ralph Lauren, etc. can be found. Look for luxurious fabrics like cashmere, silk, mohair, angora, crushed velvet, and soft wools. If some items aren't perfect, simple adjustments can be made. Replace ugly buttons; clip out shoulder pads (save them to tape around the shoulder ends of hangers for increased support of heavy or stretchy garments); take in side seams of too large items; remove dreary linings from otherwise translucent or lightweight apparel; turn tops with unappealing necklines backwards so that you have a ballet-neckline, which gives a shoulder-broadening look. Use a black marker to darken a worn or faded spot on dark garb or white chalk or powder to camouflage a small stain in light-color fabric. Cashmere, mohair, and angora sweaters can be hand-washed and then rinsed in water which contains a quarter-cup of glycerin (for softness and drape). By buying at these charity shops, you will be a supporter of a worthy cause, get good quality merchandise, and save money for your appreciating assets, jewels.

Jewelry represents one of your most important personal expressions of individuality and idea of aesthetic allure. You can use jewels to add instant oomph, to give vibrancy, to provide a point of interest that sets off an article of clothing. A piece or set of jewelry can make your whole outfit look fashion forward or ultra feminine. Antique and collectible jewelry is what gives mass-produced clothing some punch; when you dress up with a bijou bauble, it boosts your spirits. Glistening gems can give you dazzle and make you feel glamorous, sensual, and playful. There is even a costume jewelry design called the "tremblant." Rhinestones are set on hidden springs which quiver as the wearer moves, resulting in sprays of sparkles and spontaneous kinetic energy. This and other types of vintage jewelry can make your energy level soar. At night, pull out all the stops by wearing shimmering dangly earrings, gleaming copper chokers, or radiant rhinestone bracelets. Jewels can provide a riot of color and eye-catching accent.

Or, for a different mood, you could choose jewelry which exults the subtle charms of history and patina. You could emphasize ethnic accomplishments by donning an exotic and enduring jeweled specimen of an era. Why not wear something superluxe, an object that you might find in a museum of historical artifacts, a jeweled symbol of a moment in time, a coveted talisman of a culture? Don't waste your money on trendy trinkets or jewelry "inspired" by vintage designs when you can invest in authentic vintage jewelry, which has withstood the test of time and become a modern classic. One primary reason for buying vintage jewelry is to develop your personal style. When you don these investment jewels, you are wearing a one-of-a-kind work of art and have developed a signature style of your own. Of course, your style goes beyond fashion and jewels, but they speak volumes about who you are and personalize the image of how you want to be perceived. And, as F. Scott Fitzgerald wrote in "Bernice Bobs Her Hair:" "When a girl feels that she's perfectly groomed and dressed, she can forget that part of her. That's charm. The more parts of yourself you can afford to forget, the more charm you have." When you feel you look good, you can relax about that part of yourself.

The following sections will relate historical background on costume, Native American, copper, and Mexican collectible and antique jewelry and ideas on how to locate them. You will want to know what sets this jewelry apart, what kinds to look for, and how to take care of each type. Then there will be photographs of the jewelry and the fashion look that can result from the combination of simple clothing and collectible jewels. You will see how easy it is to achieve a polished appearance, and how your vintage jewelry can be enjoyed both as an investment and as a piece of wearable art.

Costume Jewelry

Until the 1920s, fine personal ornamentation of gold and precious gems was made exclusively for the noble and the elite. Jewelry had been an unmistakable indicator of social status. There was a wide gap between high society's fine jewels and the homemade (using materials such as clothespins, marbles, wood, cloth) or dime store jewelry of those with less money. But then advances in industrialization allowed the manufacturing of jewelry which simulated genuine jewels and also created a burgeoning job market so that they could be afforded. A rapidly evolving mercantile class contributed to a democratization of tastes and values. Simultaneously, a mass immigration of talented European artisans to America was occurring because of the encroachment of World War II in their own countries. This confluence of events caused the disparate social distinctions in the wearing of jewels to disappear. From the 1920s on, reasonably priced costume jewelry started to be worn by the newly moneyed middle-class and it appeared very similar to that which had previously adorned only the very wealthy.

The term "costume jewelry" refers to the first jewelry specifically designed to provide a finishing touch for an ensemble and to be manufactured for the general public. Even casual dresses were designed with intricate detail, and they were each accompanied with the "cleverly chosen etceteras" of hat, gloves, handbag, and jewelry (the whole matching she-bang was called a "costume"). Because of austerity restrictions on fabrics needed for the war effort, dresses became shorter and less voluminous, and an emphasis was placed on accessories. The popularity of costume jewelry actually began in the 1920s and '30s with the sanction of trend-setting designers Coco Chanel and her rival Elsa Schiaparelli. Both had an impeccable sense of fashion and produced unparalleled seasonal collections. Couturier Chanel invented the bias cut, drop-waist, and non-frilly linear silhouettes for her chic, classic fashion creations and liberating sports wear. Although her clothing featured unencumbered conservative lines, her jewelry feminized the garments with elegant but flamboyant fake jewelry. She is often pictured bedecked with prodigious amounts of pear-shaped simulated pearls, strands of carved beads, long gilt chains, massive brooches, and rows of bracelets set with multicolored faux cabochon gemstones. She wore by day that which previously had only been considered appropriate for evening wear.

Schiaparelli was inspired by and collaborated with famous artists like Giacometti, Jean Cocteau, and Salvador Dali in the design of her fabric patterns. She was the first to translate *trompe l'oeil* — a style of painting in which objects are depicted with realistic accuracy — through fabric print and embroidery. For one dress, a Grecian urn was embroidered on the fabric and filled with silk roses. On another, an embroidered hand clutching a real sequined scarf was stitched across a garment. Dali's influence was seen as a pair of huge, red satin lips which had been sewn onto a sequined coat. Schiaparelli's deliberately unorthodox fashion motifs featured ripped fabric and safety pin clasps. Her innovative jewelry designs were also daringly fanciful, shockingly bold, and inspired by Art Deco (motifs consisting of simple geometric forms such as the square, triangle, and circle and combined to create abstract arrangements), Surrealism (the practice of using fantastic imagery to produce unnatural juxtapositions), and Dadaism (deliberate negation of traditional artistic values). There were necklaces hung with pea pods or colored metal zodiac signs, earrings shaped like hands or telephones, brooches and buttons depicting lovebirds, lobsters, or lampposts. Both Chanel's and Schiaparelli's accomplishments were intended for the privileged clientele of society, but the designers had an enormous effect on jewelry manufacturing because they made costume jewelry incontestably acceptable.

During the late 1930s, many established designers of fine jewelry immigrated to New York and Rhode Island (the historical center of American costume jewelry) because of the advent of WWII in Europe. Famed jewelry designers such as Marcel Boucher of Cartier, Hobé, and Alfred Philippe from Paris, who had been used to working with gold and precious gems, relocated to America. Fashion proved indestructible even during those tumultuous times. The artists started their own enterprises or joined established compa-

Glittery jewels are now being worn night and day. Rhinestones are dazzling for ritzy occasions; full-on brilliants boost dressy clothes into something spectacular. For casual outings such as a trip to the grocery store, taking the kids to a soccer game, or going out for a pizza on a Friday night, wear a bejeweled bug brooch on a T-shirt or some twinkling bracelets on your wrists. You can even wear rhinestones with jeans, but only dark denim — be it Earl or Old Navy — will do. Dark denim will give an upscale backdrop for your faceted stones. Keep jeans pristine by never laundering them. If a catastrophe happens, use a home dry cleaning kit or send them out to be cleaned. Then, wear those fabulous fakes and shine. Who doesn't need a little sparkle in their life?

nies such as Trifari. Much of the design and craftsmanship of costume jewelry during this period was the result of these designers who were forced by circumstances to adapt their skills to downscale materials such as sterling, rhinestones, glass, and enamels. Rhinestones are machine-made, diamond-cut stones, which were imitations of natural colorless quartz, stones found along the banks of the Rhine River. The natural stones, washed down from the Swiss Alps, had long been used in jewelry and sold in tourist shops. In the early twentieth century, Bohemian glassmakers started producing artificial clear gemstones to simulate the natural stones. They were well-received, demand rose overseas, and a foreign importer listed them as "rhinestones" on shipping manifests. For these transplanted designers it was an economic necessity to produce costume jewelry. These famous European designers, true artists, created heirloom quality jewelry while using affordable, available materials.

In looking at selected costume jewelry, it is apparent that the workmanship is no less than that of jewelry wrought in gold and precious gems. Even when mass production revolutionized the industry, many designers refused to lower their standards. They insisted on intricate hand-cast work with sterling and base metals (instead of with gold), Austria's finest simulated gemstones (considered superior because of their extremely high lead content), and quality finishing techniques. A quote by Mimi de Nascemi, a well-known costume jewelry designer, sums up the appeal of costume jewelry. She wrote:

An original design is not a novelty, it's worth infinitely more than that; it's a minor work of art. I adore costume jewelry but I do not enjoy a flashy novelty. The philosophy of transiency is a merchandising and advertising gimmick. It's not true workmanship or an artisan's type of activity. Someone who really works at something seriously puts a tremendous amount of effort and love into it. . . It doesn't matter if the material is precious or not, it's what the artisan does with the material that counts. My jewelry is polished, enameled, finished, refined and put together by hand after the molding process. It has an 'investment' feel about it. Costume jewelry is so indicative of the moment in time it is created. It evolves because, although the criteria for making the product remain the same, the interpretation of the product changes with the evolution of the era. Costume jewelry becomes a marvelous reflection of the time. Since glass, plastic, tin and other materials are not as expensive as precious metal and real jewels, they allow the designer to exaggerate a bit and be more lavish without fear of exceeding the purchaser's budget. The designer can be more au courant and expressive of the period. Collectors enjoy jewelry from the past because it is truly a mirror of the moment. Humankind has always sought adornment, and costume jewelry is not as expensive as precious metals and stones and is an art form that will never die.

Beginning in the 1930s, an enormous influence on American lifestyle was the emulation of Hollywood's major motion picture stars. Paris had been the center of fashion for centuries but now Hollywood provided the consummate visual medium for setting and disseminating trends. This influence is just as strong today as it was in the 1930s.

Consider the immense popularity of the tabloids, *Instyle, Us,* and *People* magazines, as well as television shows such as "E, Entertainment" and "Entertainment Tonight." The "Hollywood effect" has been felt since the earliest days of moviemaking. One way the average person could attain the glitzy glamour of filmdom was to wear jewelry similar to that portrayed on the screen. This innocent imitation was done in the heyday of costume jewelry (1930s – 1950s) by the middle class majority, by blue-blooded socialites, and even in their real lives, by the movie stars themselves.

Several top-notch designers enjoyed the success of their products within the entertainment sector. Designer Joseff of Hollywood supplied costume jewelry for historical drama and epic films, also for 1970s and '80s television shows such as "Murder, She Wrote," "Dynasty," and "Mission: Impossible." Stars such as Carole Lombard and Joan Crawford personally bought the Joseff jewelry sold at the most exclusive shops. Jean Harlow's appreciation of fabulous fakes was well known to those who saw her in films and in movie magazines where she wore masses of it. Bette Davis and Marilyn Monroe had a penchant for Schreiner jewelry and frequently wore it in the 1950s. Hobé jewelry was featured on actress Maureen O'Hara in "The Wings of Eagles," an MGM movie made in 1957. The Hobé Company used movie stars to advertise its jewelry and coupled

After slipping the stem of a brooch through the fabric of your garment, slide a small plastic, short tube (purchased at any bead supply store) onto the stem just before the clasp. Secure the clasp. This will insure that the pin won't fall off should the clasp come undone.

Wear your brooches on the shoulder opposite from your seatbelt strap when you're driving. Seat belt shoulder straps can scratch or dislodge stones and pearls. Some of the colors, sizes, and shapes of old stones may be difficult or impossible to replace.

their pictures with the slogan, "Jewels of legendary splendor." Another costume jewelry producer, Kenneth J. Lane, designed jewelry for Elizabeth Taylor, as well as for the Duchess of Windsor, Nancy Reagan, Jacqueline Onassis, and Ivana Trump.

By reading various books on costume jewelry, you can learn which designers and manufacturers wrought quality jewelry. You might limit yourself exclusively to signed (stamps on the backs of jewelry which identify the maker or designer) pieces, at least until you are more knowledgeable about the field. Some of the designers who were active during the years 1925 to 1975 and known for their quality work were Boucher, Caviness, Chanel, Ciner, Coro, Christian Dior, DeMario, Eisenberg, Florenza, Haskell, Hobé, Hollycraft, Joseff, Kramer, Kenneth J. Lane, Napier, Oscar de la Renta, Regency, Renoir, Robert, Schiaparelli, Trifari, Vendome, and Weiss.

With time and experience you will probably gravitate to the designers whose work you like the best. A collector eventually learns that each designer's work can be identified by his or her own particular personal style: Schiaparelli for her unorthodox, surreal designs; Eisenberg and Swarovski for their superior stones; Vendome for unusual beads and the ubiquitous fleur de lys (the term applies to the jewelers' mark for the city of Verdun, France — it literally means flower of light, is a symbol of life and power, and conceptualizes the shape of the iris) end-piece; Miriam Haskell for her baroque pearls, use of wired beads, and burnished brass; Florenza for its Victorian appearance; Hollycraft for its multitude of pastel rhinestones and date mark; Hobé for its Byzantine flair and use of semiprecious stones; and Weiss for its high-quality crystals. There is such variety in

Many necklaces tend to be in the "choker" style so popular in the '40s and '50s. If you prefer a little longer look, add an extender to the necklace. Make the extenders out of pieces of gold or silver colored chain and add clasps and "O" rings to the chains with jewelry tools. You need about a three-inch piece of chain, then attach the clasp to one end of the chain and the "O" ring to the other. Clip the extender onto the ends of the necklace. Your hair will cover the extended chain, provided that you have hair long enough to cover the back of your neck. The extender will cause the necklace to hang just a bit lower on the neck, elongating it. All components of extenders can be found at any jewelry supply store.

Another trick to both lengthen and modernize the look is to take a necklace which was made to be worn double-stranded and simply wear it as a single strand with the decorative endpiece (not the clasp end) hanging down. Many designers such as Vendome and Hobé used elaborate end-pieces. The visual effect of this technique is of a long strand of necklace with an eye-catching, dangling drop at the end.

costume jewelry that there is surely a style to suit every taste.

Where You Can Find Costume Jewelry

You can find costume jewelry at antique shops, antique and gem shows, street fairs, Junior League shops, vintage clothing stores, flea markets (arrive early when the vendors are setting up for the best selection), church bazaars, garage (go to the wealthiest areas of your city, they will usually have the best stash) or tag sales, local auctions, estate sales, and, if they'll part with it, from other collectors. Read trade papers such as the *Antique Trader* or classified ads to find auctions which specialize in jewelry. One of the best places to find vintage jewelry is a shop which is sponsored by a charity. My personal favorite is the Discovery shops of the American Cancer Society (for information on locations, call 800-227-2345 or on the Internet, www.cancer.org). In addition to usually being available, vintage jewelry is specially accumulated for an annual sale at each of the shops. Additionally, for a more global marketplace, you can find costume jewelry on the Internet under eBay.com. Look under "Costume Jewelry," then enter the name of the designer or manufacturer you're looking for.

For additional information, you can try www.jewelcollect.org. This site is an excellent portal to all kinds of costume jewelry, price guides, repairing techniques, and historical information. Also:

Lucille Tempesta
VFCJ (Vintage Fashion and Costume Jewelry)
P.O. Box 265
Glen Oaks, NY 11004
(718) 939-3095/Fax (718) 939-7988

Rhumba!
Terri Friedman
P.O. Box 148186
Chicago, IL 60614-8186
(773) 929-9007

Care of Costume Jewelry

Costume jewelry is very fragile. Never allow any moisture on your piece or immerse it in water, especially if it has rhinestones. Water will dull the stones and may even lead to "dead" stones — those with no brilliance or depth. How you care for your jewelry will determine its continued beauty. Costume jewelry needs to be protected. Do not just throw it in with other jewelry in a big tangle. If you have found a piece in excellent condition, know that a caring conservator has protected it for many years. Continue the stewardship of your lovely piece of art. Place each jewel in acid-free tissue paper and place in a single layer in a shallow storage box. Keep your jewelry at a moderate, constant temperature.

To clean rhinestone jewelry, hold it upside down and dip a soft toothbrush or Q-tip in isopropyl alcohol, then tap off the excess. Gently rotate the brush around all the stones. When finished cleaning, lay the piece upside down on a clean towel to dry for about 15 minutes. Allow plenty of time to dry. When dry, examine the jewel and repeat the cleaning steps if necessary.

Hollycraft Corp. bracelet, c. 1954. Blue and pink rhinestones surround a large purple/blue "art glass" stone in six starburst shapes. $95.00 – 115.00.

Enamel, chatons (small round cut stones), and marquise cut rhinestones comprise this imaginative Alice Caviness apple brooch. C. 1950s. $60.00 – 85.00. Private collection.

Ciner faux pearl necklace with alternating pavé rhinestone and gold metal frontispiece design, featuring large drop pearl. $75.00 – 95.00.

The iridescent rainbow effect of the rhinestones called "aurora borealis" was popularized in 1953. The process involved vacuum-plating various metals onto the glass. This prong-set Listner necklace was manufactured in the 1950s of faceted citrine-colored stones. $65.00 – 90.00. Author's collection.

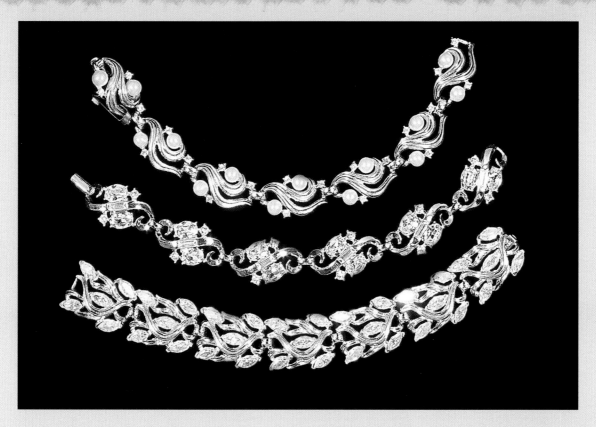

Three Trifari rhinestone and gold metal bracelets of different designs, each with matching earrings (not shown). C. 1940. $95.00 – 130.00 set. Author's collection.

These are the same bracelets as above. This is an example of why background foils (clothes) need to be simple. The pattern of this fabric design obscures the beauty of the pieces of jewelry.

Unmarked green and blue faceted rhinestone brooch with fuchsia art glass central stone. C. 1960s. $185.00 – 225.00. Author's collection.

Karen wearing brooch above with teal colored sweater and white flat-front, side-zip pants. Good shopping, or movie going outfit.

Christian Dior necklace and earring set. Teardrop-shaped pearls with pavé rhinestones give this an Art Deco look. C. 1970s. $175.00 – 225.00. Author's collection.

Exquisite Trifari aurora borealis and green rhinestone bracelet and pin set. All stones are flawless and prong-set. Although impossible to see in a two-dimensional picture, each piece of jewelry has a second, raised layer of stones. Even clasp on bracelet has an inlaid rectangular stone. $200.00 – 225.00. Author's collection.

"Navette"-cut, fuchsia-colored stones form a swirling pattern for this Weiss brooch and earring set. C. 1950s. $175.00 – 225.00.

Kristin wears a twin set with white pants and sandals. A relaxed outfit to wear to lunch or dinner on a summery day.

This set features teardrop-shaped opalescent and carved, leaf-shaped stones with pearls and faceted rhinestones, all prong-set. By Kramer of New York. C. 1950s. $150.00 – 200.00 set. Author's collection.

DeMario brooch clearly calls for simple clothes and a ritzy occasion. Gilded metal with baroque and seed pearl design is reminiscent of Miriam Haskell's pieces. C. 1940s. $175.00 – 200.00. Private collection.

Weiss butterfly brooches. Violet brooch has japanned (a process of darkening wire by immersing it into a black by-product of coal) metal and frosted rhinestones. Blue and green rhinestone brooch with citrine cabochon accents. All rhinestones are prong-set. C. 1950s. $125.00 – 150.00 each. Author's collection.

Schiaparelli parure with large blue cabochons in wide bracelet and necklace. Sterling, dangling earrings complete the parure. $450.00 – 550.00. Author's collection.

Is there anything that could possibly perk up the exuberance of a Pucci print with its unexpected patterns and vibrant colors? Yes! In a word — Schiaparelli. Both are classics and will always be in style.

Here Melissa, Kristin, and Sara dress up plain white cotton T-shirts with various jewels, showing that jewels can look right at home with simple clothes.

Florenza brooch features graceful swirls of celadon-colored art glass. The central stone has colored interior particles which change colors as the viewer shifts the brooch's position. C. 1950s. $175.00 – 225.00. Author's collection.

Plain white top and celadon-colored pants look fine but lack a point of interest.

Just the addition of the Florenza brooch and a coordinating sweater really makes a big difference in the excitement level of the outfit.

23

Want to call attention to your face? This brooch will do it.

A Regency faceted rhinestone brooch which features prong-set, marquise cut rhinestones in an assortment of shades of very light to dark gray. Brooch is 6" long. $135.00 – 175.00.

Celadon parure looks stunning when worn with black. Not much beats a basic black background which enhances the beauty of any jewel.

This Coro parure of necklace, bracelet, and earrings alternates celadon-colored chaton, prong-set stones. C. 1960s. $225.00 – 265.00. Author's collection.

Karen wearing matching beige cashmere turtleneck and warm fringed shawl.

The Hobé double-strand agate necklace worn as a single-strand. This method lowers the focus of interest which flatters tall women.

Sara in the long strand of tortoise glass cubes and Melissa wearing the double-strand agate, pearl, and crystal necklace/earring set. Both women wear their jewels with classic black.

Hobé glass cubes in tortoise shell coloration with matching earrings. Necklace has a small gold rose for its clasp. $150.00 – 200.00 set. Author's collection.

Hobé double-strand necklace and earring set of banded agate, pearls, and green crystals, bought in its original leather box. The necklace can be worn either in the intended double strand to accentuate the face or as a single strand, with the gorgeous end-piece hanging down. $250.00 – 300.00 in original box. Author's collection.

Kristin uses the brooch to secure a shawl which leaves her arms free to hold her husband's arm or carry a bag.

Unmarked faux watermelon tourmalines (a semiprecious natural stone) in brooch and earring forms. All iridescent stones are prong-set and the center stones are domed with scalloped edges. $95.00 – 125.00 set. Author's collection.

Sara uses the brooch to accent her tiny waist and pick up the color of her dress. One of the beauties of watermelon tourmalines is the array of colors they project.

Either bracelet could be worn with this simple summer outfit.

Jacques Hobé, master craftsman and the foremost jeweler in Paris, started to manufacture fine jewelry at affordable prices in 1889. The excellence of his design was not diminished by the use of downscale materials. He employed exquisite casting, stamping of metal, and handset-ornamental gemstones. He knew that women wanted their jewelry to be beautiful whether it was made of precious materials or not. His son William came to America and had a following of Hollywood stars. These bracelets reflect the company's attention to detail. C. 1950s. Bracelets, $150.00 – 225.00 each. Author's collection.

This detailed Weiss necklace is decidedly dressy. The company's jewelry is comparable to Eisenberg jewelry with excellent Austrian rhinestones of exceptional quality. C. 1950. $95.00 – 120.00. Author's collection.

All the jewelry you need to wear for an evening out and about is this Weiss necklace.

A pin this heavy needs a bulky fabric to hold it properly. Here, it is pinned to a sand-colored suede jacket. A black turtleneck sweater and black pants complete the outfit.

If you buy an unmarked set like this one, you want to look for indicators of fine workmanship such as intricate metal work, prong-set sparkling stones (in this case, aurora borealis), and eye-catching designs. The set features crescents piled upon crescents of prong-set stones. The set is so vibrant that a progressively darker filter had to be used to dull its appearance for this photograph. A large and impressive set. $175.00 – 225.00 set. Private collection.

Traditional Trifari gold and pearl necklaces in imaginatively different designs. C. 1960s. $75.00 – 100.00 each. Author's collection.

The gold necklace really stands out against a dark olive green sweater and skirt. A good outfit for going to the theatre.

Miriam Haskell at her finest. Meticulously hand assembled with intricate beading, prong-set rhinestones, and exquisite metalwork. Truly a piece of art. C. 1940s. $225.00 – 265.00. Author's collection.

Miriam Haskell baroque pearl and gilt metal necklace and Maltese brooch. C. 1940s. Necklace, $175.00 – 225.00; brooch, $165.00 – 200.00. Private collection.

Kristin wears the set with a pink blouse and black pants on her way to a San Francisco club for dinner and dancing.

Overlapping disc-shaped clusters of crystals form a glittering design. This "va va voom" set is by Vendome. Vendome was a subsidiary of Coro and was promoted as their superior line of jewelry. $185.00 – 225.00. Author's collection.

Florenza pendant with rhinestones and opalescent teardrop glass stones. Like all Florenza jewelry, this has a distinct Victorian appearance. C. 1940s. $85.00 – 125.00. Author's collection.

This delicate Florenza necklace suits Jeannie's fine features.

Shades of slate-colored Austrian crystals and rhodium (a platinum alloy which has been electroplated on metal) form this Eisenberg set. C. 1960s. $195.00 – 225.00 set.

The colors of the set play perfectly on a classic wool jumper. This outfit could be worn to the office or for an afternoon at the opera.

Our lady in red, Sara, wears the bracelet with reptile skin slides.

Hollycraft bracelet, stamped 1953, displays red, pink, green, and clear sparkling stones set in meticulously stamped metalwork. $95.00 – 115.00.

Marked (but illegible) salamander brooch of superb design. The salamander was once believed to thrive in fire without harm and symbolizes passion. C. 1940s. $300.00 – 400.00. Author's collection.

A splurge but worth it for the fit, designer jeans and jacket provide a subtle background for a salamander.

Melissa wears this set with a silver tank and pant outfit for a special evening out.

Trifari faux turquoise and rhinestone necklace and earring set. C. 1950s. $225.00 – 265.00 set. Author's collection.

Very rare Oscar de la Renta brooch, featuring intricate design and pavé rhinestones. C. 1960s. $350.00 – 400.00. Author's collection.

Marcel Boucher brooches. Left to right: Narcissus flower, $65.00 – 75.00; pavé petal flower pin with pearl center, $175.00 – 195.00; carved ivory brooch, $65.00 – 85.00. These small flowers would add a point of interest to any top or jacket.

Costume Jewelry

Two double strand Vendome necklace and ear-ring sets of varied pink and peach stones and crystals. Identifying fleur de lys end-pieces are clearly visible and also look lovely hanging down from a single strand. Here both necklaces are worn together. $105.00 – 135.00 set.

42

One of the double strand Vendome necklaces and earring sets is worn with a more casual outfit.

Kristin, looking elegant and feminine.

Eye-appealing design of gold metal and rhine-stones for this delicate Trifari necklace and earring set. Feminine when worn with a dressed down twin set or with a fur-collared sweater for evening. C. 1960s. $175.00 – 225.00.

This is a 1950s Trifari interpretation of the late nineteenth century chatelaine. It was considered an indispensable part of a woman's dress. A chatelaine was a silver or gold brooch composed of chains and clasps which held accoutrements such as house keys, pencil, perfume vial, shoe button hook, thimble, needle holder, letter opener, card case, cross, spectacle case, whistle and/or snuff box. The item required two belt hooks to support its weight. Some of the finest were made of gold and set with precious gems. It was the precursor of the twentieth century carry-all, the handbag. Trifari's rendition is collectible and wearable because of its deep red, blue, and green cabochons, reminiscent of Chanel's costume jewelry. $105.00 – 125.00. Author's collection.

A fringed square of cashmere is a splurge but it is a classic, can be worn in all seasons, and keeps you warm. This outfit would go to the opera or a big city dinner.

Native American Jewelry

When you think of Native American jewelry, what generally comes to mind is silver jewelry with turquoise stones. Of course, other traditional embellishments include coral, malachite, lapis lazuli, shell, and jet, but the vast majority of antique Indian jewelry was fashioned with turquoise. Indian legend has it that turquoise is a sacred talisman, brings good fortune, insures a long, healthful life, and is a gift from the gods. Turquoise has been called "the gem of the centuries" and is so revered that the stones have been passed from generation to generation of Native Americans as family heirlooms. The most highly prized turquoise comes from certain identifiable mines (different types of turquoise are named after the mines from which they were quarried) and raises the value of the jewelry which contain it.

Although the name "turquoise" comes from the French word for Turkish — the stone was long imported to Europe from Turkey — the name is misleading because the imported gem actually originated from Persian mines. The most ancient of harvested stones, turquoise has been used as ornamentation for more than eight thousand years. One of the earliest amulets known is a turquoise and gold bracelet which has adorned the arm of the mummy of Queen Zer of Egypt for 8,500 years. The oldest known mines were in the Sinai Peninsula, with Egyptian and Persian mines following close behind. Turquoise is found in only a few places on earth which include arid regions where copper or iron-rich groundwater seeps into cracks in rocks. It occurs as veins, nodules, and lime-encrusted stalactite projections either on or close to the surface of the earth. A stone's degree of blueness is achieved by the amount of copper contained within it, while the degree of greenness depends upon the amount of iron it gradually garnered. Only 10% of the turquoise being mined today is gem grade. What determines gem quality is the deepness of the color and the hardness of the stone (which allows it to be polished to a high luster). Now most turquoise is low-grade chalk-stone, which is dyed or treated with oil or resin to deepen the color and stabilized to make the stone hard enough to work with. Gem-quality natural turquoise is still being produced in Iran and China, and in only one mine in the United States, the Sleeping Beauty Mine in Arizona.

The manufacturing of American turquoise jewelry began in New Mexico, was probably established by 900 A.D., and eventually used in trade to the Mayans, Aztecs, and Incas. The Cerrillos area, located just south of Santa Fe, was the largest known source of turquoise on the continent. The semiprecious stone it produced was used extensively for ornamental and monetary purposes. Between 900 – 1150 A.D., Indian miners manually broke an estimated one hundred thousand tons of rocks with stone axes and picks. Then these laborers, bearing heavy leather bags of raw ore on their backs, climbed up vertical shafts on notched logs to bring the rock to the surface for processing. Vast quantities of the turquoise nuggets were sent throughout Central America and all the way down to the Mayan cities of Chichen Itza and Tulum in the Yucatan. It has been told that the Aztec emperor Montezuma wore jewelry from the remote Cerrillos turquoise mines. Of course, the stones were also widely distributed locally. Over fifty thousand prehistoric artifacts of Cerrillos turquoise fashioned into pendants, beads, rings, and disc mosaics were found as a result of a twentieth century archaeological excavation in Chaco Canyon, New Mexico. Ancient Indians highly prized turquoise as their most valuable form of adornment.

Southwestern Indian tribes had used copious amounts of turquoise ornamentation for centuries, but around 1850, a Navajo changed the form of Native American jewelry making forever. Seeking a way to make a living, Atsidi Sani journeyed south to a border Mexican town where he persuaded a local blacksmith to teach him how to make utilitarian metal (iron, copper, brass) items such as knives and bridle bits. He expanded his abilities and started to fashion buttons, rings, earrings, and bridle ornaments. He subsequently taught these skills to fellow Navajo friends, and it was not long before they engaged in buying United States and Mexican silver coins (silver was not mined by native tribes) to produce ornamental silverwork. As early as 1870, the Indians used the melted down coins to form ingots which were cooled and hammered on pieces of train rail, tree stumps or large stones into thin sheets of silver. These sheets were then trimmed down to the desired size and shape and stamped with crude punches which had been copied from Mexican leather patterns.

In the early 1900s turquoise and silver started to be combined in Native American jewelry. The innovation conveniently coincided with the coming of the railroad, a revolutionary method of transportation which resulted in a

> *Never hesitate to mingle Native American jewelry with Mexican pieces. Their long-standing exchange of techniques, characteristic styles of art, and cultural histories are so intertwined that you can mix and match without fear of offending the fashion police.*

tremendous increase in tourism. Tourists to the Southwest wanted souvenirs symbolic of the native population, namely silver and turquoise jewelry. The Indians scrambled to try to meet the demand. By this time, the differing tribes, Navajo, Zuni, and Hopi, had developed their own distinctive styles. The Navajos had taught silversmithing to the Zunis around 1872, and the Hopis learned from the Zunis early in the 1900s. Navajo jewelry emphasized heavy silverwork and large turquoise stones. It was a bold art form which featured symmetrical designs and used turquoise gemstones as complements to the metal.

Zuni designs were characterized by extraordinary lapidary skills (skills of gem cutting) which were employed to achieve closely set cabochons in row upon row of same-sized turquoise stones (called needlepoint or petit point design). The use of many small stones was especially significant while silverwork was secondary. Zunis were the first to sign their jewelry. Favored Hopi techniques involved cutting designs in one layer of silver, then joining it with a bottom layer of solid silver by pressing or soldering the layers together. The lower layer was then darkened by oxidation; the top layer was polished to a high sheen. Hopi work seldom used gemstones, and the design was usually geometrical. All three beautiful jewelry styles were extensively used as "old pawn" in the early twentieth century.

The term "old pawn" describes early Native American handmade jewelry which was originally intended for personal use, but later had to be pawned. Jewelry can be called "old pawn" if the transaction occurred between 1890 and 1940. Indian jewelry was an asset with a known value that could be pawned at trading posts. There it could be traded for a partial sum of its worth in cash or goods. Old pawn was the working collateral of its day. Indians wore their wealth in the form of jewelry and would pay for everyday necessities with a blue turquoise stone bracelet or a concha (Spanish for shell) belt of heavy silver ovals. If the pawn was not retrieved within a certain time, it was sold by the trader. This almost never happened, so revered was the jewelry by the Indian for its connotation of wealth and prestige and for its use in ceremonies. When the sellers came into some cash (usually from sale of a rug or wool from a sheared sheep), they would come back and redeem their treasure. Although Native American jewelry was venerated by the Indian and coveted by tourists, its appeal was primarily limited to the Southwest.

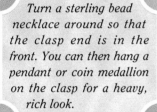

Turn a sterling bead necklace around so that the clasp end is in the front. You can then hang a pendant or coin medallion on the clasp for a heavy, rich look.

By the 1960s and '70s, just when most of New Mexico's turquoise mines had been exhausted of ore, there was a piqued interest and increased demand for Indian jewelry. Its popularity was soaring when *The Wall Street Journal* proclaimed that the gemstone was equivalent to diamonds as a sure investment. In 1972, a *New York Post* fashion article gushed, "It looks as if the American Indians are ready to take back Manhattan." When you see the originality of design and the skilled craftsmanship of antique and collectible Native American jewelry, you will understand its appeal. In addition to beauty, the jewelry expresses their reverence for life and the environment. Indian storytellers tell of the creation of all natural things: the mountains, the planets, and all living beings. Each main Native American jewelry style translates this love of nature into symbolic design: a massive Navajo concha belt with repetitive patterns of bear claws or feathers on scalloped-edged silver and sometimes dotted with turquoise inlay; a beautiful Zuni bracelet formed of tiny, brilliant blue stones embedded in silver like a mosaic of stars; or a Hopi necklace simply embellished with geometric depictions of perhaps prehistoric petroglyphs, water waves, buffalo, or the sun. These styles are nonverbal expressions of a culture. Because of its intrinsic beauty, superb quality, and spiritual significance, Native American jewelry should remain esteemed as wearable art for a long time to come.

Where You Can Find Native American Jewelry

Authentic, handmade Indian jewelry is increasingly appreciated by discriminating consumers. Photographs of Christie Brinkley in a Got Milk? advertisement and of Sally Taylor (James Taylor and Carly Simon's daughter) in an *Us* magazine article featured the celebrities wearing their own Native American jewels. Old pawn handmade jewelry is disappearing from the market. Various museums and collectors as far away as the Middle East retain most of it. The most valuable of this type was made prior to WWII. Often it is just an educated guess as to whether or not a piece is actually old pawn. It might be easier to identify jewelry by its silversmith than try to pinpoint a specific time when the jewelry was made. To determine its age, expert appraisers look at the cut of the turquoise stone and at the silver-work. Was the silver hand pounded or filed; was it composed of ingot or coin silver? Also helpful is evaluating the craftsmanship of the jewel by looking for symmetry of decorative detailing. If the jewelry is absolutely symmetrical, it is probably not handmade. Eventually, traders and those involved in the marketing of native jewelry wanted artisans to identify their work. Artists started stamping their work in about 1950, so if you come upon an unmarked piece, it was probably made before then.

For our purposes, old pawn or antique handmade and Native American jewelry crafted through the 1970s would qualify as investment jewelry. Admittedly, the year 1980 is an arbitrary cut-off date for Native American jewelry. It is a viable art form although the effects of the lucrative business of Indian casinos on this time-consuming skill is still to be seen and continues to metamorphose in its technique. Most importantly, deal only with shapes of high reputation. Needless to say, you can find Native American jewelry in the beautiful state of New Mexico (turquoise is the state gem). You can find shops located in any city by looking in the Yellow Pages under "Indian goods." You can also research Native American jewelry on the website www.ebay.com. Try flea markets, estate sales, auctions, antique stores, and gem shows.

Find a dealer (a person or a store) whom you trust and ask him to call you with anything he thinks might interest you. The best collections are a collaboration between you and your agent because he knows just what you're interested in. Think of the dealer as your personal jewelry stylist, a person whose eye for quality keeps you returning time and again, one who has a good reputation and repeat customers. He will sometimes show you things before he shows anyone else. He will already have done exhausting and extensive legwork, spent time picking through lots of jewelry, and eschewed lots of dreck. When you get together with your agent, you can choose the créme de la créme from his expert culling efforts.

Here are several sources that you might try if you are interested in both old pawn and contemporary Native American jewelry.

Joe Goure	Lynn Trusell	Hoshoni
Betty's House of Turquoise	Crown and Eagle Antiques	309 East 9th St.
815 Sutter Street	P.O. Box 181	New York, NY 10003
Folsom, CA 95819	New Hope, PA 18938	(212) 674-3120
(916) 351-9326	(215) 794-7972	
	www.crowneagle.com	

The Annual Indian Market, which has been held in Santa Fe, New Mexico, every August since 1922.

Care of Native American Jewelry

Be sure to treat your turquoise with care. The stone is extremely porous and can turn color or darken with perspiration, oil, make-up, perfume, dishwater, hand lotion, or temperature changes. Turquoise scratches easily. Because it is a natural porous stone which needs air circulation, do not store in plastic; rather, store it in a soft cloth pouch. Use only "Wadding polish," which comes in a can, to polish your Native American jewelry. The polish is made in various countries, including the United States, Canada, England, and France. After use, cap the can tightly to avoid evaporation of the cleaning chemicals which are contained in the polish. You can even use this polish on porous stones; it will produce a lustrous hue on turquoise, coral, and jade. You could also use a silver polishing cloth but use it to clean only the silver of a piece, as it may discolor any stones.

For the excellent repair of American Indian jewelry as well as for purchasing beautiful contemporary Zuni jewelry, you may contact:

Marcia Martinez
Sweet Feather, Inc.
224 S. Main St.
Yuma, AZ 85364
(520) 373-2262
(520) 305-1011

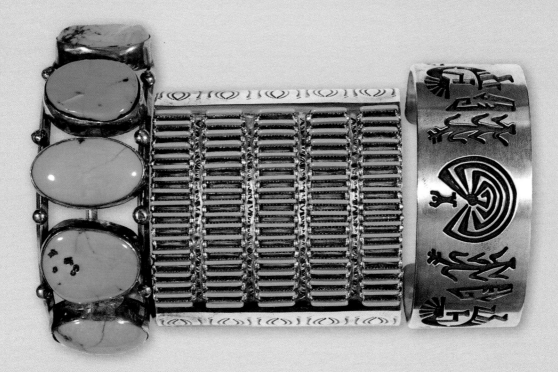

These bracelets show the different Navajo, Zuni, and Hopi techniques. From left to right: Navajo bracelet with five large turquoise stones, $350.00; Zuni bracelet, $525.00; Hopi bracelet, $250.00. Courtesy Betty's House of Turquoise.

Large Navajo bracelet with substantial emphasis on the beauty of the turquoise stone. $600.00. Courtesy Betty's House of Turquoise.

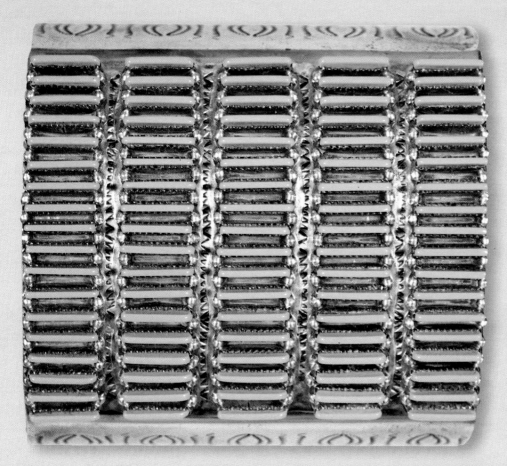

Wide Zuni cuff bracelet in needlepoint design, with repetitive scalloped motif stamped in sterling on both sides. $525.00. Courtesy Betty's House of Turquoise.

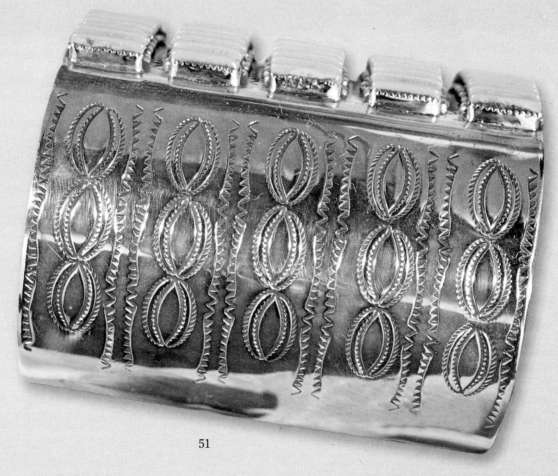

This is a particularly fabulous
Zuni fetish necklace. There are five large, hand-
carved turquoise images of bears and buffalo and many smaller
images of birds, owls, foxes, squirrels, frogs, and rams along the necklace
sides. This type of fetish necklace has been made since prehistoric times. A fetish of a carved
animal is supposed to contain that animal's strength and power, and if treated well, will transfer that
power to its owner. $1,200.00 – 1,500.00. Private collection.

This fetish necklace can indeed be worn outside of Santa Fe. Yes, everywhere — to the office, to the local theatre, or to dinner.

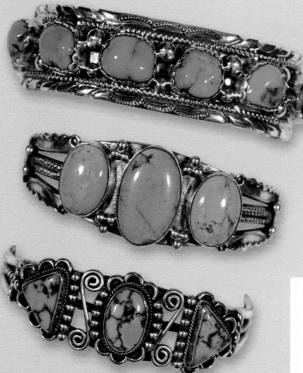

Navajo bracelets, all unmarked, feature stamped designs and wire and bead overlay. Different turquoise mines are represented by various matrixes and shades of the turquoise stones. $250.00 each. Author's collection.

Only the bracelets and ring on the right hand are Native American antiques. The color combination of the rose silk Chinese jacket and turquoise (most turquoise now comes from China) bracelets is stunning.

The cultural combination is appropriate because, as Mary Davis in her book *Mexican Jewelry* points out: "There is a great similarity in the art style and working techniques in...Mexico and China." Native Americans later learned their techniques from the Mexicans.

The following several pages present a bevy of necklaces which show the bounty of Native American imagination and ingenuity. First, a Zuni necklace with petit point medallion by artist Harvey Begay. Harvey Begay is the son of master silversmith Kenneth Begay who began learning the trade in the 1930s. This bracelet is c. 1970s. $1,000.00 – 1,200.00. Private collection.

Navajo squash blossom necklace with naja, a central hanging pendant. C. 1970s. $1,000.00 – 1,200.00. Private collection.

Zuni inlay turquoise and coral necklace in mosaic design with hinged medallion. $795.00. Courtesy Betty's House of Turquoise.

Navajo necklace with large turquoise medallion, sterling leaves, and stamped bail. $1,400.00. Courtesy Betty's House of Turquoise.

Navajo old pawn, square-cut turquoise stone squash blossom necklace. $1,400.00. Courtesy Betty's House of Turquoise.

Beautiful squash blossom necklace with large turquoise blue stones. $1,500.00. Courtesy Betty's House of Turquoise.

Old pawn squash blossom necklace with horseshoe-shaped naja, the central hanging pendant. Early Spanish influence is seen on the tips of the crescent shape. The small button endings were first used on horse bridles as an amulet to protect against "the evil eye." $1,400.00. Courtesy Betty's House of Turquoise.

Very heavy Navajo coin necklace, with domed silver dollar medallions, coin beads, and turquoise nugget naja. C. 1950s. Though this necklace is unmarked, those involved in marketing native jewelry increasingly wanted artisans to mark their work both for identification and economic purposes. However, this practice didn't commence until around the 1950s. $800.00 – 900.00. Private collection.

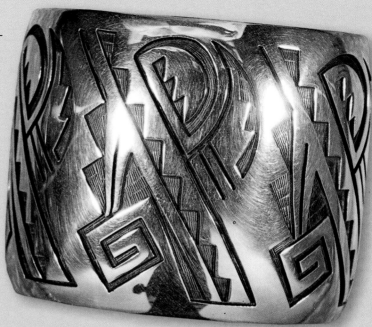

Strong geometric design demonstrates overlay and chisel work in this wide Navajo cuff bracelet. $350.00. Courtesy Betty's House of Turquoise.

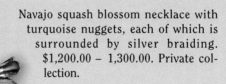

Navajo squash blossom necklace with turquoise nuggets, each of which is surrounded by silver braiding. $1,200.00 – 1,300.00. Private collection.

It is not uncommon for members of one tribe to utilize the techniques of another to make jewelry. Navajo Jake Livingston has used the Zuni inlay technique to create this stunning parure of necklace, earrings, bracelet, and ring (not shown). $3,700.00. Private collection.

Huge Navajo cuff bracelet with fluted silver and flower head design. C. 1960s. $995.00. Courtesy Betty's House of Turquoise.

Navajo dapped (metal hammered into a dome shape) silver dollar and dime bead necklace. Coin silver is 90% silver and 10% copper. $400.00 – 500.00. Author's collection.

Silver worn with gray is a pleasing pairing. Three different Native American bead necklaces combined here, one of which is worn with clasp ends in front. A sterling medallion, cast from silver found on the Spanish sunken ship, the *Atocha*, is hung on the clasp ends. Because of the long-standing and culturally intermixed histories of Native America, Mexico, and Spain, their jewelry can be combined with impunity.

Toward the end of our photo shoot, the husbands of our models came to pick them up. We included Sara's husband Jeff in this picture of her wearing the Benally bracelet.

A Benally deep-red coral bracelet, using shadow-box technique with deep oxidized (blackened) recesses. $250.00 – 300.00. Author's collection.

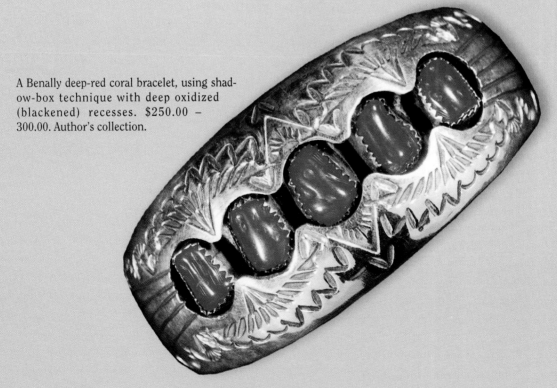

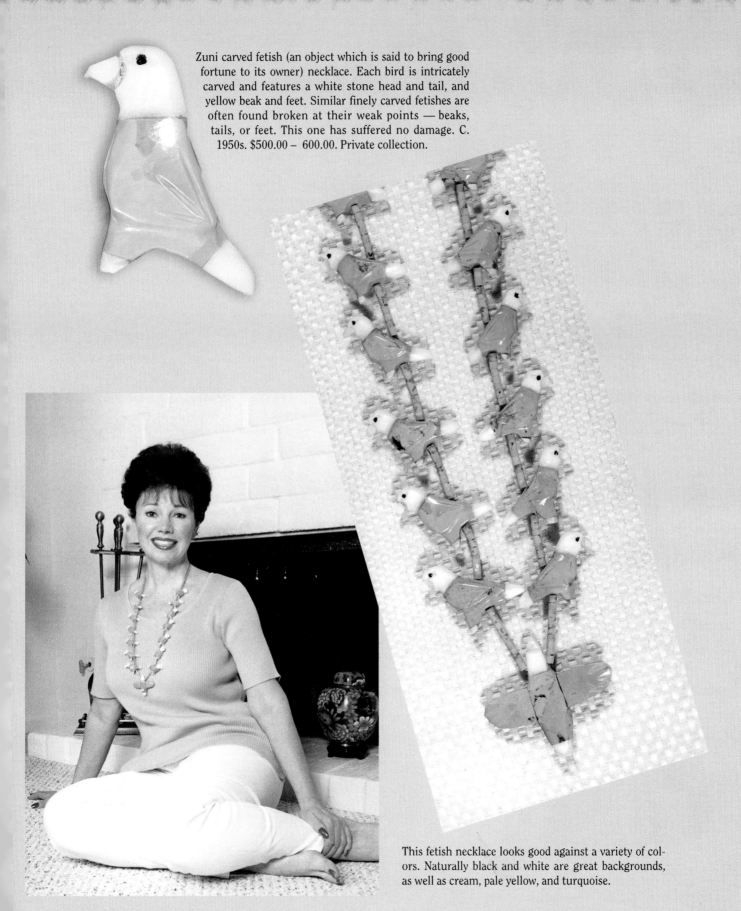

Zuni carved fetish (an object which is said to bring good fortune to its owner) necklace. Each bird is intricately carved and features a white stone head and tail, and yellow beak and feet. Similar finely carved fetishes are often found broken at their weak points — beaks, tails, or feet. This one has suffered no damage. C. 1950s. $500.00 – 600.00. Private collection.

This fetish necklace looks good against a variety of colors. Naturally black and white are great backgrounds, as well as cream, pale yellow, and turquoise.

Gorgeous Zuni cluster (cluster technique began in the 1920s) bracelet on sterling support wire backing and soldered-on silver beads and braiding. C. 1950s. $525.00 – 595.00. Author's collection.

Native American summer.

Greenish turquoise/sterling Navajo bracelet. Older turquoise that may have been repeatedly exposed to urban pollution or extreme temperature changes can develop cracks, as can be seen in the large, central stone. Not marked. C. 1940s. $175.00 – 195.00. Author's collection.

Early cluster bracelet on right and newer Navajo wide cuff bracelet on left. The newer bracelet has two nicely colored turquoise stones on a sterling band. $250.00 – 450.00 each. Private collection.

A sand-cast, early Navajo bracelet with seven turquoise nuggets on sterling background. Not marked. $250.00 – 300.00. Author's collection.

A Native American winter look, complete with Indian dance shawl.

Sterling bracelet and ring with scrimshawed fossilized walrus ivory cabochons. Walrus ivory is not used much now; instead caribou antler, which is naturally shed, is preferred. Bracelet created by Navajo Tom Morris. Ring was created by Navajo Virginia Piaso. Unknown value because of uniqueness of set. Author's collection.

Beige, black, or white would be good background colors for this unique set. Keep clothes simple so that the art is the focus.

66

This Navajo bracelet was bought from a gentleman whose father had worked for the Atchison, Topeka and Sante Fe Railroad. The man, his mother, and siblings could ride the route for free and did so on all their vacations. He remembers stopping at Harvey House restaurants in the 1930s and '40s as a child. In those days many Harvey Houses dotted the railroad line and offered culinary hospitality for travelers. Founder Frederick Henry Harvey exclusively hired comely young women to serve the food. These women were required to sign a contract not to marry for a year. They were strictly supervised, lived in special dormitories, and had nightly curfews. Harvey Houses offered Indian crafts such as blankets, baskets, and jewelry for sale in their gift shops. This bracelet was specifically made for tourists and was bought at a Harvey House by the gentleman's mother in the 1930s. Priceless. Author's collection.

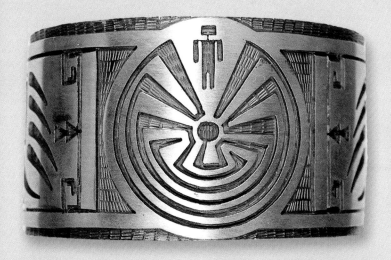

Hopi cuff bracelets using overlay technique. Overlay design is made by cutting a pattern out of one piece of silver and soldering it onto another plain piece of silver. The bracelet is then oxidized with liver of sulfate to produce a dark shading. The top layer is polished to a high sheen. This distinctive style began in 1947, when the federal government funded programs to train Hopi GIs, fresh from WWII, to be able to earn a livelihood after the war. $250.00 each. Courtesy Betty's House of Turquoise.

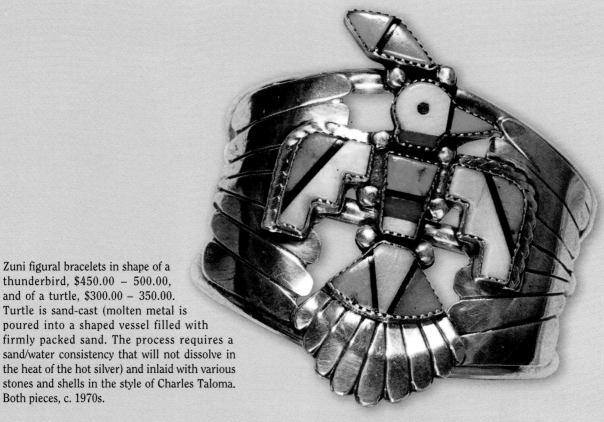

Zuni figural bracelets in shape of a thunderbird, $450.00 – 500.00, and of a turtle, $300.00 – 350.00. Turtle is sand-cast (molten metal is poured into a shaped vessel filled with firmly packed sand. The process requires a sand/water consistency that will not dissolve in the heat of the hot silver) and inlaid with various stones and shells in the style of Charles Taloma. Both pieces, c. 1970s.

Unusual Navajo pink mussel shell bracelet. $250.00 – 350.00. Author's collection.

Looks like a summery accessory to me. Hot weather, light-weight white pants and simple top should do the trick.

This Navajo bracelet, with its two huge and heavy hunks (I call it the "boulder bracelet") of turquoise, was bought at a gallery/restaurant gift shop in the 1960s. $600.00 – 800.00. Private collection.

Three Navajo bracelets, from the top: Greenish cluster stone bracelet. C. 1940s or '50s. $400.00 – 500.00; natural Lander blue turquoise stone bracelet which won a prize at one of Santa Fe's annual Indian Markets. $600.00 – 800.00; turquoise nugget bracelet uses shadow-box technique to enhance the turquoise (which is artificially colored), $250.00 – 300.00. Private collection.

Navajo bracelet with center silver strip. Inlay and overlay techniques employed for this 1970s unmarked piece. $500.00. Private collection.

Side view of Navajo bracelet.

Navajo mother-of-pearl leaf and turquoise necklace and bracelet set made in the 1960s. Ramon Latero, when he worked for the Luthy shop, was the first to employ the leaf motif in Native American jewelry. Set is unsigned. $1,500.00 – 2,000.00. Private collection.

Zuni coral bracelet and necklace set. The Pueblo of Zuni are located in western New Mexico, south of Gallup, near the Arizona border. Jewelry making is the major industry of the Pueblo and their craftwork is vitally important to their economic survival. The Zunis are famous for their lapidary skills as well as channel inlay, cluster work, needlepoint, and petit point. $1,500.00 – 2,000.00. Private collection.

A large Horace Iule (1901 – 1978) cross. Zuni Iule would draw patterns on common stone, carve out the patterns, and then pour hot silver into the hollowed area. Iule concentrated exclusively on making variously sized and decorated crosses. Many artists' families pass traditional designs and equipment down through generations to make their product immediately identifiable. Horace's children still use his casting equipment to make "Iule" crosses. This is one of his later pieces, as evidenced by the ornate embellishment as opposed to his earlier, starker pieces. C. 1970s. $500.00. Private collection.

A smaller cross, marked "H. Iule." $200.00 – 300.00. Author's collection.

Navajo sterling bracelet with cabochon squares of onyx. Unusual choice of stone. C. 1970s. $375.00 – 425.00. Private collection.

Side view of the bracelet shows stamped scalloped design on bezel settings which provide a base for the three stone squares.

Copper Jewelry

A huge crater has been carved out of a mountainside in the jungles of the island of New Guinea. The sight of the Grasberg open pit mine is appalling, like a gigantic gaping wound. Modern day mining is not a popular industry because it causes such damage to the earth in order to extract ores. The pit contains one of the world's largest deposits of copper and the site has incurred vigorous protests from environmental activists all over the world who have tried to halt the cruel exploitation of Mother Earth. (Of course, the mining of all metals results in the destruction of the earth's lithosphere, so let us reduce our need for it by recycling, reviving, reusing!) Because the price of commodities is at an all-time low, the continuation of the mine is in jeopardy. But while copper production dwindles and more environmental restrictions requiring costly reclamation projects are enforced, our need for the metal continues. Today, copper is used in the electronics industry, roofing, water pipes, coinage, exclusive cookware, insecticide compounds, and even in cosmetics.

The name "copper" was derived from a mine on the Greek island of Cyprus. In Greek, Cyprus was called Kypos. Philosopher and scientist Pliny called copper "aes Cyprium" because the oldest and largest deposits were found on the island of Cyprus. Copper is believed to have been the first metal known to mankind. Neolithic civilizations fashioned ornaments such as links and beads, as well as tools and weapons from the metal. Archaeologists have found examples of copper bracelets, anklets, headbands, and hair clasps in ancient burial sites. In Turkey, copper clothing ornaments dating back to 5,000 B.C. have been unearthed. Copper was the metal of choice during the Arts and Crafts crusade of the early 1900s. Its artistic shift endorsed skilled handcrafting and rejected the devil "dehumanizing machines." The movement began by marrying Middle Age-inspired motifs with a pre-industrial level of superb technique. Although it is seldom used any more for decorative items such as vases, tiered serving trays, candlestick holders, cigarette boxes, ashtrays, serving platters, sculptures, or jewelry, during the 1930s – mid 1960s such usage was favorable and affordable. Specifically the use of copper in jewelry brought out the design potential of inexpensive materials to create beautiful art for the common man.

Those who prize the burnished beauty of copper and its jewelry's original design and exquisite craftsmanship have been attracted to the work of two men who were outstanding in their art: Francisco Rebajes of Rebajes and Jerry Fels of Renoir/Matisse of California. Rebajes was an immensely impressionable man who kept almost exclusive company with other artists in his community. In 1932 he began to create jewelry using borrowed tools and aluminum cans in a basement apartment in New York City. On the opposite coast, Jerry Fels began his career in 1945 out of economic necessity to support his Los Angeles-based family. Both contributed to the heritage of metalworking and created large-scale businesses for the manufacturing of copper jewelry, as well as other objects they designed and produced.

Francisco "the Sponge" Rebajes soaked up the omnipresent sources of aesthetic expression of New York's artists, intellectuals, and poets. His conceptualizations reflected Brancusi, Picasso, and the Arts and Crafts Movement. A gamut of artistic styles including geometric, abstract, classic, and cubist configurations affected his work. Some motifs were derived from nature and represented fish and butterflies, flowers and branches, fauna, and the bodies of humans. Rebajes' artistic entrancement extended to exotic cultures and primitive art, examples of which are seen in his pre-Columbian figures, Grecian heads, and African pachyderms. Even trends in commercial and industrial design were reflected in his amazingly comprehensive influences. He often replicated the hand-hammered look of antique pieces and sometimes incorporated crystals, abalone, hematite, amethyst, pearls, or tiger-eyes into his work. That he was able to combine these prolific inspirations with the unerring technical economy is certainly a tribute to his genius. The involvement of Rebajes' fertile imagination and the soul of an artist are apparent in each piece of his production. He set the standard for copper art jewelry in the 1930s and '40s.

Rebajes was the consummate Bohemian artist whose life work became an artistic and financial success. Because his jewelry bridged the wide division between adornments of precious metals and gems and trinket-type tokens and because of the beauty of his unique jewels, Rebajes' business enterprise thrived. He progressed to larger and larger workshops and finer storefronts. At his entrepreneurial apex, Rebajes had his

Wear copper in multiples, gathered together with a common theme. Multicolored enameled leaf pins, parures of earrings. bracelet, and necklace, or pieces with similar geometric configurations look good when combined. Trios (or more) in copper are not overwhelming, over-the-top, or ostentatious. They, like several complementary pictures on a wall or a collection of similar items displayed on a table, look best when grouped together.

jewelry featured in fashion magazines and in the finest department stores. He was so successful that his shop in Greenwich Village generated a million dollars a year in retail sales, and he later moved to a swanky area on Fifth Avenue in New York. His work was shown in the Metropolitan Museum of Art, the National Museum of Design, and the Cooper-Hewitt Museum of the Smithsonian Institute. Rebajes retired in the early 1960s, but he left a legacy of an unparalleled caliber of artistry and technical excellence and established a new perception of copper in jewelry that is still prized today.

Another company which manufactured copper jewelry was founded in Los Angeles in 1946 by Jerry Fels, called Renoir of California. He chose the name "Renoir" (Renoir's Impressionist paintings exhibit recurrent themes of romance and leisure) to demonstrate his intent to manufacture wearable art which incorporated high aesthetic design. Symbols of fine art, music, and theater were often used. He was also influenced by contemporary abstract and modern artists like Kandinsky and Miro. Nature's forms were often represented and expressed with literal or figurative interpretation. The shapes of microscopic life like amoeba and other organic forms show the extent of the concepts which he conveyed in copper. These and other designs were eventually mass-produced in Fels' production studio employing local Mexican metal smiths. Southern California's influential Crafts Guild awarded honors to Fels for his designs.

Renoir jewelry became very successful and was sold through a network of salesmen to upscale stores and boutiques. His work was advertised extensively in fashion magazines such as *Glamour* and *Vogue*. Fels started manufacturing copper jewelry with surface enamel work in 1952. He named this line Matisse. The use of enamel decoration on metal originated in ancient times. The technique involved using a thin layer of ground glass which was made into a paste, applied to one side of a metal, and then fired at a high heat so that the two were fused. Enamels required one or two firings of temperatures in excess of 1500°F. The technical aspects of working with a thin layer of glass made Matisse jewelry more expensive and difficult to manufacture. The glass and metal had different cooling times after firing, which often resulted in the destruction of the delicate enamels. Fels' solution was to also enamel the entire backs of pieces to create an equal tension on the front and back during the cooling process. Called "counter enameling," the enamel was applied to the back first, then to the enamel front and finally fired. Counter enameling and deliberate pre-kiln doming (metal naturally domes in high heat) of the copper prevented the problematic movement which had previously caused chipping and cracking. Rich deep colors required several thin layers of enamel with firing after each layer. After firing, the piece would finally be pickled (a weak sulfuric acid was applied to remove unwanted debris) and polished. All these steps were time-consuming and costly but resulted in the quality product that Fels demanded.

Fels combined the qualities of pragmatist, great designer, and perfectionist; he was also very much a humanitarian. Endearingly he assigned a name to each of his designs as if naming a child, surely an expression of his great passion. Among the names were Diana, Nocturne, Basketweave, Scultura, Starburst, Vortex, Coronet, Solitude, Nouveau, Laurel, Nefertiti, Guinevere, Barcarolle, Seine, Palette, Rondele, Lido, Espana, Evening, Cleopatra, Parisien, Dance, Rhythm, Surf, Textura, Geo, Grecian, Trellis, Polaris, Orient, Galaxy, Echo, Fantasy, Lagoon, Bayou, and Glade. Because he had heard tales of copper's healing powers for the pain of arthritis and rheumatism, Fels made individual pieces upon request for those individuals who were afflicted. The Renoir/Matisse line closed in 1964.

For a custom look to long-sleeved tops and sweaters, turn your garment inside out. Fold the sleeve in half with the seam as one border. Then sew the wrist end of a sleeve together, about an inch in (depending on your wrist size) from the seam. Sewing in a diagonal toward the upper part of the sleeve, taper the sewn area into an elongated triangle. The apex of the triangular-sewn shape should be about three inches up the seam of the sleeve. This takes just ten minutes or so and will eliminate the bunching of fabric from between the ends of your cuff or hinged bracelet. It will also prevent the sleeve from covering your bracelets.

Where You Can Find Copper Jewelry

For investment purposes, I recommend concentrating on signed copper jewelry only. As part of the manufacturing process, a large percentage of Fels' output included his trademark names stamped on each piece. The Matisse and Renoir jewelry was signed in geometric script prior to 1954. To avoid imitation by other copper jewelry manufacturers, Fels had his designs copyrighted in 1954. After that date, he marked his jewelry in either a script or block style. Rebajes' jewels were marked in a geometric script featuring a unique "s" shaped like a horizontal eight at the end of his name. Fels' and Rebajes' marks/signs can be found on clasps, on the backs of earrings, pins, and necklaces, or stamped on the outside of some cuff bracelets. These signed copper jewelry items are of greatest interest to collectors.

This beautiful jewelry is becoming increasingly rare. You can still frequent antique shows and shops, estate sales, flea markets, and period shows (Art Deco, Fifties, etc.) where there are certain to be sellers who have copper pieces. It is such a thrill to find matching parts of a set or parure in different locations. Finding earrings to match a necklace or the discovery of a bracelet whose design duplicates a pair of earrings you already own is actually quite possible. In fact, I once bought a Rebajes bracelet in Sacramento, California, and found matching earrings in a small shop in Santa Fe, New Mexico.

You can also go on the Internet. Go to www.ebay.com, then to "costume jewelry" and search "Rebajes" or "Renoir" or "Matisse Renoir." I encourage actual examination of a piece before you buy because condition is so important, but going online can give you a price range as well as a larger selection for the copper jewelry that you are interested in.

Care of Copper Jewelry

In his heydey, Rebajes' forte was fine design and sage business acumen. But today most of his jewelry has a darker brown appearance than does Fels' because the formulation that Rebajes used to protect his products against tarnishing was basically not as well researched as that of the technical perfectionist Fels. Although many people like an aged, oxidized look, you may prefer a more burnished gleam. Simply polish the jewelry with a silver polishing cloth for shine and then place the piece into a small plastic zippered bag to avoid re-tarnishing.

Fels proudly advertised his products' durable finish and carefree maintenance. To keep his copper jewelry glowing, he needed to use a superior lacquer formulation which he eventually found in a small local chemical company. The sealant was trade-named Copron. After each piece was created, it was given a thorough cleaning, sulfuric anodizing, and polishing. Copron, specifically formulated for Fels' jewelry, was a clear coating of water-baked enamel that was then fired onto each completed piece. It has kept Renoir jewels tarnish-free for more than fifty years. So there is not much to do to care for Renoir and Matisse jewelry. Just buy in top condition and protect in sealable plastic bags. Don't attempt to restore your jewelry by removing varnish or re-anodizing it. Look for signed pieces in fine condition or don't buy it.

Sara and Melissa, both dressed in dark colors to provide impact for the burnished beauty of copper.

Copper Jewelry

The Vortex and Basketweave bracelet and earrings worn by Sara in the page 77 photograph. Basketweave cuff bracelet, $55.00 – 85.00, earrings, $45.00 – 65.00; hinged Vortex bracelet, $75.00 – 125.00.

The geometric design and link size of the Park Avenue necklace and earrings combine well with a double-square bracelet. C. 1940s. Park Avenue necklace, $85.00 – 125.00; matching earrings, $45.00 – 65.00. Double-square linked bracelet, $85.00 – 115.00. All jewelry by Renoir.

Leaf by Matisse/Renoir. Enameled pin and earring sets in maple leaf design. As many as five successive firings were required to achieve these luminous iridescent colors of enamel on copper. C. 1950s. Pins, $85.00 – 125.00; earrings, $45.00 – 75.00. Author's collection.

Simple sweater provides a casual background for Matisse/Renoir pins.

Copper jewelry can be worn in doubles or triples without causing concern about being too ostentatious.

Hawaii by Matisse/Renoir. Pin, $65.00
– 95.00; earrings, $45.00 – 65.00.
Author's collection.

Bracelet and earring set of unknown design. Stamped Renoir. Bracelet, $65.00 – 85.00; earrings, $45.00 –
65.00. C. 1940s. Author's collection.

Clockwise from upper left: bracelet and earrings in double coil design; bracelet in alternating elevated slats called See-Saw; and bracelet and earring set in Flame design. All marked Renoir. Bracelets, $75.00 – 95.00 each; earrings, $45.00 – 65.00. Author's collection.

Leaflet, accented with bent copper wire, by Matisse/Renoir. Pin, $85.00 – 125.00; earrings, $45.00 – 75.00. Author's collection.

Jeannie wears the Leaflet brooch and earring set on a white turtleneck.

Exotic Brazilian Mask brooch and earrings by Rebajes. Brooch,
$75.00 – 125.00; earrings, $50.00 – 60.00. Author's collection.

Hand-cast brooch by Rebajes represents
a heavily veined leaf with berries.
Brooch, $150.00 – 185.00. C. 1930s.
Private collection.

This vintage Scottish
Pringle cashmere
sweater, embroidered
with heavy beading, had
languished for months at
a consignment shop. The
reason was apparent: the
"gold" plating on its buttons and the central part
of the beaded motif had
eroded to an uneven, tarnished metal color. But upon
close inspection, I noticed that the vast majority of the
beadwork was very beautiful and was a burnished brown
color that would look great with copper. First the buttons
had to come off and be replaced with new copper buttons,
which would echo the color of the intended copper jewels. Then, to blend the new buttons with the bead motif, a
button was sewn right on top of the existing beading —
in the center of each "flower" shape, front and back. Now,
some may say that combining an ornate, heavily beaded
sweater with any kind of jewelry would be a flagrant case
of "gilding the lily." But one thing for sure, you would
never see this outfit on anyone else!

On Karen's right wrist and on ears, the Basketweave
set by Renoir. Bracelet, $55.00 – 85.00; earrings,
$45.00 – 65.00. On her left wrist is an African-
inspired motif bracelet by Rebajes, $75.00 – 150.00.

The next three sets of Matisse/Renoir necklaces and earrings are different colored variations on a theme. Blue Evening set: necklace, $95.00 – 145.00; earrings, $45.00 – 75.00. Author's collection.

Green Seine set: necklace, $95.00 – 145.00; earrings, $45.00 – 75.00. Author's collection.

Pink Laurel set (earrings not shown):
necklace, $95.00 – 145.00; earrings,
$45.00 – 75.00. Author's collection.

Renoir Parisien necklace, $125.00 – 165.00.

Renoir design reminiscent of a blending of an autumn leaf and Tahiti motif, $85.00 – 125.00.

Grecian parure in perfect condition, thanks to Copron which prevented tarnishing. Marked Renoir. Earrings, $45.00 – 65.00; bracelet, $75.00 – 85.00; necklace, $95.00 – 135.00. Author's collection.

Vortex and Parisien bracelets on arm on the left. Both are hinged, $125.00 – 195.00 each. See-Saw, Basketweave, and slanted slat bracelets on arm on the right. All three are cuff style, $65.00 – 95.00 each. All bracelets by Renoir.

Left: Parisien bracelet and earring set of ball-bearing-shaped design, $125.00 – 195.00. Right: Vortex design bracelet of swirling crescent shapes, $125.00 – 195.00.

Bracelets really stand out against basic black or rich brown.

Jeannie wears the architectural Peter Pan design with a red leather jacket and buttery yellow turtleneck and slacks — a very artsy combination. Fels would approve!

Peter Pan parure by Matisse/Renoir. The enamels on these pieces required repeated firings of up to 1500°F to join glass powder and metal. Necklace, $95.00 – 145.00; bracelet, $65.00 – 95.00; earrings, $45.00 – 75.00.

Top bracelet looks like Sari with two large round disks. Hinged bracelet, $85.00 – 125.00. Bottom cuff bracelet is called the Scarab motif, $85.00 – 105.00.

Gracelet set was named after Grace, a jewelry buyer who helped make the design popular. Marked Matisse/Renoir. Bangle bracelet, $85.00 – 135.00; earrings, $45.00 – 75.00. Author's collection.

Gold and copper colors of the cuff bracelet pick up the same hues in this jacket. Even better than the spring white top and pants worn here would be an autumnal olivewood-colored background to make the bracelet's gleam even more noticeable.

Rare cuff bracelet with gold/copper-colored plaques on a copper mesh background. Tapestry cuff bracelet, $115.00 – 135.00.

Nefertiti necklace and bracelet. Copper shavings were dropped on enamel powder to produce a metallic accented surface. Marked Matisse/Renoir. Necklace, $125.00 – 145.00; bracelet, $75.00 – 95.00.

Karen wears the Nefertiti set with a metallic copper sweater and dark brown pants to go to dinner with friends.

Kristin wears the Nefertiti set with a black turtleneck and black skirt to the office.

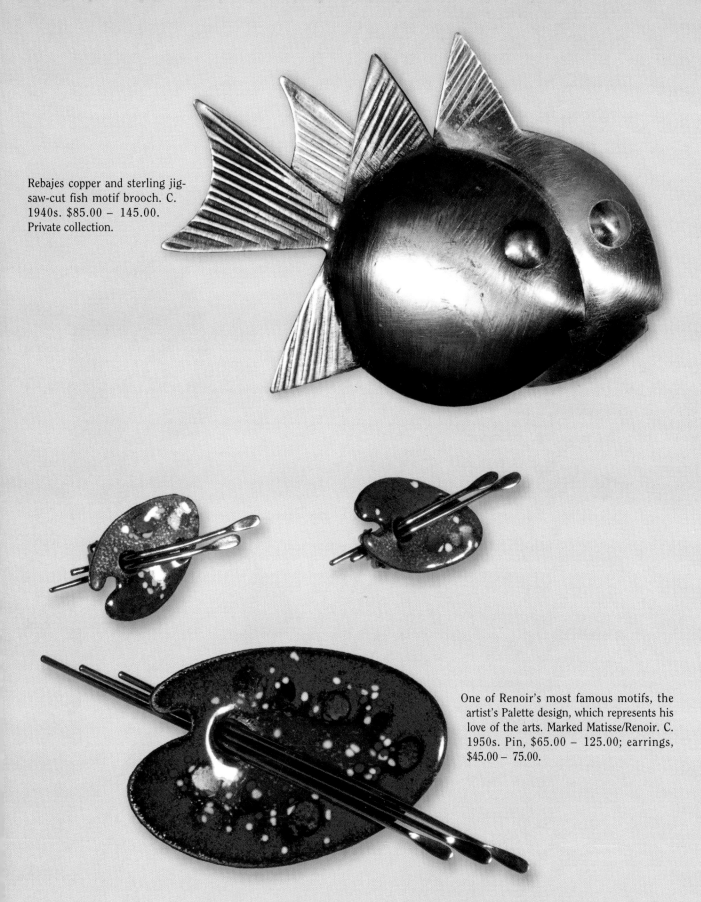

Rebajes copper and sterling jig-saw-cut fish motif brooch. C. 1940s. $85.00 – 145.00. Private collection.

One of Renoir's most famous motifs, the artist's Palette design, which represents his love of the arts. Marked Matisse/Renoir. C. 1950s. Pin, $65.00 – 125.00; earrings, $45.00 – 75.00.

Leaf shapes with coiled stems on a Rebajes pendant suspended by a heavy copper chain. Necklace, $125.00 – 165.00. Author's collection.

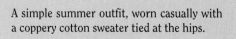

A simple summer outfit, worn casually with a coppery cotton sweater tied at the hips.

Rebajes necklace, $85.00 – 125.00, and earrings, $50.00 – 100.00.

Three hinged bracelets, all marked Renoir. Only the top bracelet design name is known as Sari. Bracelets, $85.00 – 125.00 each.

Very delicate and feminine necklace, marked Renoir. Necklace, $125.00 – 165.00. Author's collection.

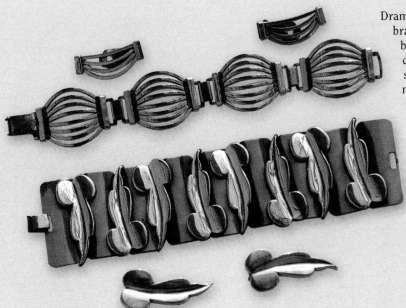

Dramatically different designs in bracelet and earring sets. Top bracelet/earring set is the design called Lagoon. Bottom set with elongated leaf motif, name unknown. Bracelets, $85.00 – 95.00; earrings, $45.00 – 65.00. Author's collection.

The Dance design by Renoir represents a limber dancer's movements. Necklace, $85.00 – 125.00; earrings, $45.00 – 65.00. Author's collection.

Mexican Jewelry

Ancient Mexico was home to many tribes which had emigrated from North and South America. The Olmec people comprised the first great civilization to settle in Mesoamerica (Mexico and northern Central America). Anthropologists believe that the ideas and craftsmanship of the Olmec provided the foundation of the cultures which followed. They were originators of the glyph (a symbol or character that conveys information nonverbally), precursor to the more advanced hieroglyphic (pictorial written language). Sculptures of monumental stone heads and jade carvings commenced with them. After the demise of the Olmec civilization, Mayan tribes migrated into Mexico during the first millennium AD. The Mayan culture became the only literate society in pre-Columbian America. Modern scholars think that Mayan hieroglyphics were one of just three writing systems in the world which were invented independently, the others being Sumerian and Chinese. Mayan kings employed scribes who wrote texts which glorified the king's reputation and established his power over his territory. These texts were indelibly inscribed as carvings on large stone stelae (pillars). Mayan hieroglyphics were also recorded on textiles, pottery, and jewelry. The last great Mesoamerican power to enter Mexico was the Aztecs, who flourished from about AD 1200 – 1521. During the period when Aztecs dominated all of Central America, neighbors making complex art surrounded them on all sides. Among these artisans were Mixtec (of Monte Alban and Mitla, communities located near present day Oaxaca) and Igualan jewelers.

Generations of Mixtec jewelers hired out as craftsmen for their Aztec employers. The Mixtecs' exquisite pre-Hispanic jewelry was constructed of gold, as well as of jade, pearls, turquoise, obsidian, and crystal. They were famous for their lapidary work, jade belts, bracelets, ear and nose plugs, and pendants (jade was always the most precious substance known to the ancient Mexicans, with its value far exceeding that of gold), gold filigree jewelry, and skillful mosaics. The Mixtecs' renowned craftsmen made ornamental mosaic masks constructed of hundreds of tiny fragments of turquoise. Some masks were built on human skulls, then the backs of the skulls were cut away to form the masks. The Igualas made a unique kind of jewelry in red, green, and yellow polished gold in the shapes of fruits and flowers. Although some silver jewelry was made, the metal almost always used for jewels was gold. This was primarily because the method employed for extracting silver was very difficult and gold was easily and abundantly found in the form of pure nuggets near riverbeds.

In 1521 Hernan Cortes, under the sponsorship of King Charles I of Spain, conquered the Aztecs. From the early sixteenth century until the Mexican revolution of 1911, Mexico was dominated by Spanish colonialism. The jewelry that was produced during these four hundred years was primarily gold filigree and exhibited strong Spanish design. There was a brief interlude between 1900 and 1911 when a pronounced movement toward jewelry made of copper occurred. The movement was inspired by the British/American Arts and Crafts period, which emphasized meticulous, handcrafted methods of fabrication. This particular copper jewelry is rare, given the few years in which it was produced, but it is historically significant as a symbol of the socialist principles that inspired the period and served as a bridge between subjugation and liberty. Then the democratic revolution, with its demands for land reform and nationalization of natural resources, finally released Mexico from European dominance. A cultural explosion followed and resulted in the renaissance of Mexico's fundamentally Indian nature. Inspired by the redeemed Olmec, Mayan, and Aztec cultures, archaeologists started researching and excavating, museums vied for pre-Hispanic art, and intellectuals wrote seriously about Mexico's venerable pre-colonial past. Even architects reanimated native themes into the concurrent Art Deco movement, its geometric abstractions heavily influenced by the lines of stepped Aztec temples, into the design of their buildings.

Mexican mines had long produced nearly a third of the silver in the world but for hundreds of years, it was exported to Spain to provide the major source of supply for Spanish coins. The refined ore was not used for the profit of the Mexican people until the early 1920s. The first men to make post-revolution Mexican silver jewelry (primarily for the new influx of curious tourists) were also heavily influenced by the renewed interest in their cultural heritage. The designs these men used for their jewelry were typical of Indian motifs, which had been artistically manipulated for millennia by pre-Hispanic artisans. Improvisations of these imperishable ancient designs were boldly displayed in the work of the descendants of Mixtec and Igualan jewelers, many of whom eventually provided the workforce for a burgeoning silver jewelry industry in Taxco. Located just south of Mexico City amidst bucolic rolling hills, Taxco originally began as a small mining settlement and progressed to being the center and soul of a new entrepreneurial enterprise.

Two Americans were significant catalysts of twentieth century interest in Mexican silver jewelry making. Frederick Davis came to Taxco in the early 1920s to work at the Sonora News Company as a news agent for all the railroads in Mexico. He traveled widely, became infatuated with the indigenous crafts of the newly emancipated nation, and started to collect them. Davis was inspired by these relics and decided to launch the first production of high-quality silver jewelry in Taxco. He insisted that the jewels be handmade by local silversmiths, which resulted in a much-needed boon to the local economy. His designs were largely responsible for the jewelry's immense popularity in the 1920s and '30s and for many of the concepts of those designers who followed him. He was instrumental in the incorporation of the stone "carved face" (small, carved stone human heads which were found by farmers while plowing their fields) jewelry that was so popular in the 1940s. After many years of promoting Mexican crafts and folk art, Davis retired in 1950. Aficionados of authentic Fred Davis handcrafted pieces value them for their appeal as wearable art. He shares responsibility with William Spratling for initiating Mexico's silver jewelry industry.

Although Taxco had been linked to Mexico City by the National Automobile Highway, in 1929 it was still an isolated mining community. This was the year that William Spratling came to Taxco on a vacation to study the town's Spanish Colonial architecture. He fell in love with the small town and conceived the idea of making silver jewelry as a way to earn a living. Spratling started a workshop with a few local young men and utilized silver and other local substances to make and sell the traditional jewelry of the region. The design ideas for his earliest pieces came primarily from pre-Columbian clay stamps, which had been used by the Indians to decorate textiles and pottery. In the workshop's early days, laborious processes were used to make these jewelry designs in silver. Thin silver blocks needed to be hammered and rolled to the proper thickness and flatness. The silver sheets could then be ornamented with piercing, repoussé (forming a pattern by beating metal up from the underside) or cutting. For decorative balls, silver wire would need to be pulled through a series of square holes of decreasing size until the correct one was reached. The wire was made into small rings, put on asbestos, and melted to form the balls. For soldering, the silversmith had to blow very hard into a curved tube, which increased the heat of a fire in a small container. In that way, he melted the solder material. He would then apply it with a fine brush where needed. For finishing a piece of jewelry, the artisan would first buff the jewel with a leaf from a special plant, which had a sandpaper-like texture. Finally, he would polish the piece to a gleaming sheen by spreading powdered pumice on his inner arm and rubbing the silver jewel against his skin.

Spratling's manufacturing techniques gradually became more mechanized, refined, and stylized, and his designs changed over the years from baroque pre-Hispanic Indian motifs to a more cosmopolitan and contemporary conceptualization. His interests expanded and he became interested in abstract modernism and Scandinavian design. He came to believe that designing was not just an inspiration but rather the result of solving a creative problem with an alternative technical method. Evolving interpretive design and skilled hand-wrought construction described his reinvigorated products. Spratling's jewelry became well known and his Mexican workshop prospered, especially during the war years when European manufacturers could not be relied upon for jewelry. Companies in the United States such as Tiffany's and Saks Fifth Avenue began to import silver jewelry from Taxco. During these peak production years, Spratling's company employed 422 workers. He established a hierarchical training system where many of his local workers progressed from being green apprentices to becoming master silversmiths. These silversmiths went on to become independent entrepreneurs who subsequently opened their own shops.

In 1939, four Castillo brothers, Antonio, Jorge (Chato), Miguel, and Justo, trained in the Spratling tradition, left to form their own workshop. The workshop, Los Castillo, became one of the largest in Taxco. They maintained high standards of craftsmanship and employed a staff of fine designers to guarantee great variety in their product. They used old and complicated techniques combined with traditional materials such as turquoise, jade, malachite, chrysoprase, or concha (iridescent abalone shell) for the manufacture of inlaid jewelry. The finished product exhibited a precision which distinguished their jewelry from all others. Their most famous and astonishing technique was called "married metals" (metales casados). A design was drawn on a sterling silver background and pieces of copper, brass, and darker silver were cut to fit the small spaces of the design. Then the metals were sweated to fit exactly so that there was no space between them, and the scant soldering material was completely invisible. The piece of jewelry appears to be made of one multicolored metal. Examples of married metals have been seen in a brooch in which a jaguar was covered with little dots of another metal no larger than a pinhead and also in a bracelet of serpent design made with extremely fine copper wire outlining small brass spots. The copper outlining was less than one thirty-second of an inch wide. The Castillo workshop employed over a hundred craftsmen who used hand tools and hand processes in creating their exquisite works of art.

Enrique Ledesma worked for both Spratling and Castillo before he opened his own shop in 1950. His designs were affected by the Modernist movement, as were the works of so many other designers of that time. However, he won special distinction and numerous prizes for inlaying stone into silver metal and shaping the materials together into a single unit which resulted in a super solid construction. A unit of silver shape was made with the desired stone encrusted into it, then polished and refined. Bracelets, brooches, and necklaces were fabricated from these units, which highlighted and emphasized the imbedded stone's beauty. His high aesthetic values were reflected by his technically flawless work, which today is appreciated as unique and original wearable art.

Hecto Aguilar started as an assistant in the Spratling workshop and moved on to become the shop's manager. He later organized his own workshop, the Taller Borda, and eventually employed over 300 craftsmen. His designs were inspired by Aztec and Mixtec architecture and other pre-Columbian art. One of his most famous pieces was a bracelet which featured alternating balls and flat areas with concealed swivel hinges. This product presented many technical problems, but his successful solution won prizes and created a durable well-designed product. In addition to his success in Taxco, Aguilar had contracts to produce jewelry for Saks Fifth Avenue, Gump's, and Neiman Marcus in the United States.

One of the most well-known silversmiths in Taxco, Antonio Pineda, also learned his craft under Spratling tutelage. His individual style was large and dramatic, although the big pieces were not heavy because they were hollow. It is technically very difficult to create the effect of mass without weight. His work incorporated costly semiprecious gemstones (those not often found in Mexican jewelry such as moonstone, chrysocolla, and topaz) and faceted gems set with as little metal touching them as possible. In 1944, his work was exhibited in San Francisco's Palace of the Legion of Honor. In 1988 he founded the Museum of Silver in Taxco, which was dedicated to all Mexican silversmiths.

There were several American women who were successful in the Taxco jewelry industry. Margot Carr, married to Antonio Castillo, originally came to Taxco to study art. After their divorce, she established her own workshop. Although she did not actually make the jewelry herself, her imaginative designs were carried out by superior local craftsmen. In contrast to other workshops and their silver jewelry, Margot de Taxco's shop products emphasized enamels on silver and masses of color. Her business card read: "Margot de Taxco. As the stars are to the night, so are jewels to the woman." Her aesthetic creations were designed to add interest and beauty to the personality of the wearer.

In the 1930s, Bernice Goodspeed began as an archaeology student interested in the motifs and rich heritage of ancient Mexico. She became a lecturer and tourist guide in Mexico City and later an author of books about the history of Mexico. Her jewelry work was characterized by her interest in pre-Columbian motifs. Goodspeed incorporated ancient polished stones and carved masks into her work, which were brought to her by farmers who had unearthed them by the dozens while plowing in country fields. Because of her jewelry's classic design and sturdy construction, Goodspeed's jewels can be worn often and in abundance without advertising "too much." Her pieces can be used for casual wear, when the same piece in gold would be too ostentatious because of its obvious worth. She is recognized for her designer's talent and her jewelry is highly collectible.

Mexican jewelry is among the most beautiful silver jewelry ever imported to the United States. Artist Georgia O'Keeffe rarely wore gold or gemstones but favored Mexican silver jewelry by Taxco artisans. She has often been photographed wearing Hector Aguilar's "X" belt (a black leather belt with broad sterling "X's" spread along the length of the belt), as well as numerous other Taxco jewels. Another devotee of Mexican jewelry is actor Diane Keaton, who can be seen in the April 2000 edition of *Reader's Digest* wearing armloads of Mexican bracelets. Despite the high quality of design and skilled workmanship that went into the making of Mexican jewelry, regretfully these treasures were not fully appreciated in their time. Although a large quantity was produced in the 1940s, much of the jewelry was melted down. There is a limited supply of antique Mexican jewelry. It is extremely collectible and has experienced a large rise in prices. Although designers' identification marks are important in determining value, even pieces of unsigned, antique Taxco jewels are expected to escalate in price.

In the early days of silver jewelry crafting, each designer or workshop had its own way of stamping jewelry to identify its designs. Although the marks often changed over the years, most conveyed information as to the workshop name, the silver content, location of its production, and sometimes a catalog or design number. For example, Spratling started off by marking his jewelry with the brand that he used on his horses. He later changed it to "WS" surrounded by the words "Spratling Taxco Mexico." Fred Davis' mark was a small "F" inside a larger "D," and Antonio Pineda's mark displayed his first name in the shape of a crown. In addition to identifying the various workshop's names (and thus its reputation), stamping informed the customer of the jewelry's silver content. For quality control, between 1946 and 1979, the Mexican government required a "quinto," the eagle (symbolic of primary natural forces and represented the revered god of the sky) assay mark on jewelry which indicated that it was authentic sterling. The silver had to contain the legal measure of at least 0.925 pure silver of which 925 parts out of 1,000 units were silver and the remaining 75 parts consisted of copper. Each piece of jewelry had to be taken to the assayer's office for weighing and then they could be struck with the eagle stamp. In 1979 the eagle mark was discontinued.

In addition to the great designers and silversmiths already mentioned, other early designers' hallmarks to look for include Lopez, Flores, Valentin Vidaurreta, Montero, Emma Melendez, Far-Fan, Sigi Pineda, Victoria, Los Ballesteros, Victor Jaimez, Villasana, and MATL.

Today, there are over 10,000 silversmiths in Taxco, and the need for governmental quality control of silver persists. This has resulted in a new marking (marks or stamps on the backs of jewelry) system. For contemporary jewelry, 1979 to the present, each silversmith is assigned a mark which consists of two letters and two numbers. The first letter denotes the city or town in which it was made: T for Taxco; M for Mexico City, etc. The next letter is the initial of the first or last name of the artist. The numbers show the position of the silversmith on the list for that particular letter. For example, if the mark is TM-13, it means that the jewelry was made in Taxco, and the artist's name — first or last — begins with M. He is the thirteenth artist to register for the letter M.

Where You Can Find Mexican Jewelry

Search antique shows and shops, gem shows, consignment stores, thrift shops, flea markets, and specialized dealers. Look in the Yellow Pages under "Antiques," "Consignment service," and "Thrift shops." Handmade signed and unsigned antique jewelry from Mexico, especially from Taxco, is worth the search.

Listed below are several places to find wonderful vintage Mexican sterling silver jewelry.

Cannery Row Antique Mall
471 Wave Street
Monterey, CA 93940
(831) 655-0264

The Glitter Box
Sheila Pamfiloff
P.O. Box 35
Walnut Creek, CA 94597
(925) 937-7554
pamfil@glitterbox.com

Mountain Lion Trading Post
Redondo Beach, CA
(310) 540-4428

Peregrine Galleries
Montecito, CA
(805) 969-9673

Care of Mexican Silver Jewelry

Before you buy, study the condition of the jewelry Use a loupe (a jeweler's magnifying eyepiece which can be found at a jewelry supply store) to decipher differing designer's marks. Obvious repairs bring down value. Check its overall appearance; the metal and stones for scratching; the tortoise or abalone shell for cracking or chipping. After purchase, keep your beautiful jewelry in sealable plastic bags to protect the silver from tarnishing (silver tarnishes in the presence of sulfur in the air). Use only a silver polishing cloth on the silver but avoid polishing the jade, obsidian, abalone, malachite, or other stones in the jewelry because the chemicals in the cloth might harm or discolor them.

Jeans and a rustic-looking alpaca jacket with rawhide binding look right with the heavy copper cuff.

A close-up of this copper cuff displays the detail of a carved stone head with elaborate headpiece and a hand-hammered copper strip laid out in geometric design. These elements fairly define the Arts and Crafts movement of the early 1900s, which urged artists to return to pre-industrial levels of superb craftsmanship. Jewelers (as well as artists in all media) were encouraged to reject the materialism that came with mass production and to investigate the design potential of inexpensive metals such as copper.

The combination of influences of the Arts and Crafts Movement and the beginnings of the Mexican Revolution were seen in many types of Mexican crafts made in the early 1900s. It was during this window in time, from around 1900 to 1911, that this copper cuff was made. In 1911 the Mexican Revolution resulted in a bitter fight for emancipation. This cuff is symbolic of an important historic transition and is one of my favorite pieces of jewelry. $400.00 – 500.00. Author's collection.

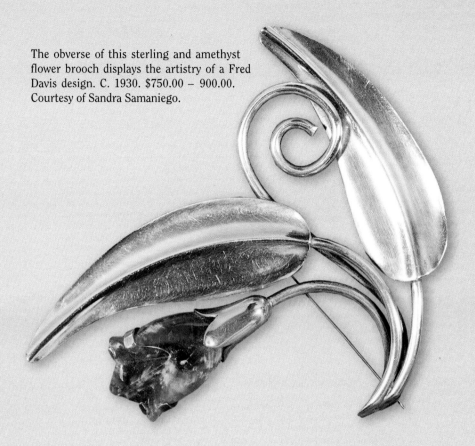

The obverse of this sterling and amethyst flower brooch displays the artistry of a Fred Davis design. C. 1930. $750.00 – 900.00. Courtesy of Sandra Samaniego.

The reverse of the brooch shows Davis' distinctive mark.

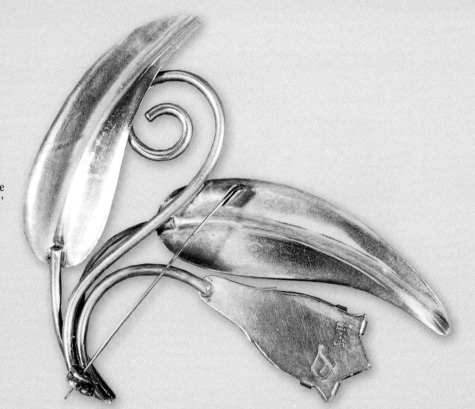

Rare green carved brooch, marked Eisenberg Original. C. 1940. $350.00 – 400.00. Courtesy of Sandra Samaniego.

If you look closely, you can see the marking, written in script, on the lower border.

Handmade sterling and amethyst bracelet. Marked Sterling, Taxco, 178, and Los Castillo. $325.00 – 375.00. Private collection.

A colorful summer shawl pulls the amethyst of the bracelets and blue of the sandals together. A simple look for a free concert in a local park or for a tropical vacation.

Sterling and amethyst link bracelets, each distinctively different in their designs. C. 1940s. $150.00 – 250.00 each. Courtesy of Sandra Samaniego.

Sterling framework and amethyst carved masks and balls design on a hinged bracelet. $300.00 – 500.00. Smaller bracelet, $150.00 – 200.00. Author's collection.

Maricela Isidro Garcia flower set of necklace and bracelet. C. 1945 – 1950. $650.00 – 700.00 set. Courtesy of Sandra Samaniego.

Sterling necklace of bangles, marked Bis. $200.00 – 250.00. Courtesy of Sandra Samaniego.

Articulated blue enameled fish necklace and earring set, marked Margot de Taxco. Made in the shop of Margot Van Voorhies. C. 1960. $700.00 – 900.00 set. Courtesy of Sandra Samaniego.

Close-up of articulated enameled fish.

Carved black onyx head and sterling bracelet, ring, and earring set, marked Taxco. C. 1950. Author's collection.

The way to wear any figural jewelry (figures with faces, animals, fish, etc.) is with its motif facing toward observers, so when the wearer's arm is extended forward, the design of a face would be plainly seen.

The Emma Melendez necklace really stands out on Melissa when she wears black, bringing attention to her face.

Emma Melendez
necklace, worn by Kristin with
white tank and leather jacket.

Emma Melendez sterling necklace. She signed her jewelry
"Emma" and gave each design an inventory number. C. 1960.
$350.00 – 400.00. Author's collection.

Blue glass stones in graceful design by
Margot de Taxco, in necklace and bracelet
set. C. 1945. $700.00 – 800.00. Courtesy of
Sandra Samaniego.

Margot de Taxco's stamp as
seen on the back side of the
necklace and bracelet.

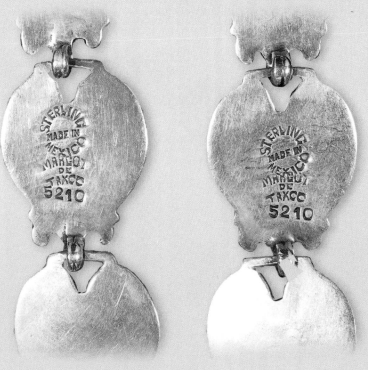

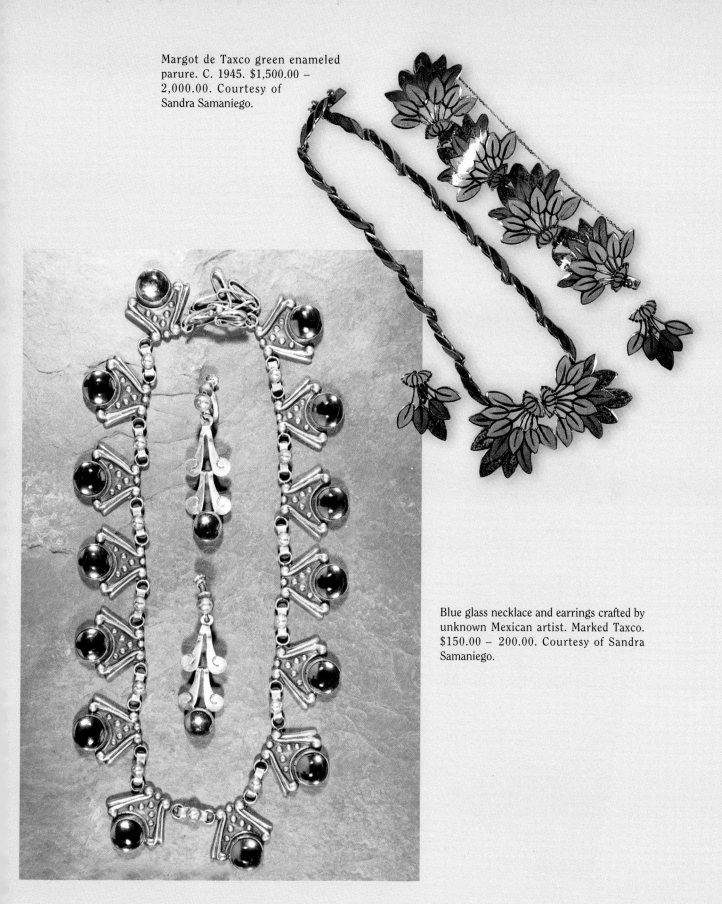

Margot de Taxco green enameled parure. C. 1945. $1,500.00 – 2,000.00. Courtesy of Sandra Samaniego.

Blue glass necklace and earrings crafted by unknown Mexican artist. Marked Taxco. $150.00 – 200.00. Courtesy of Sandra Samaniego.

Hand-carved jade and sterling bracelet, marked Sterling and P.Y. Miocico. $250.00 – 350.00. Unattributed jade brooch, marked Taxco. $150.00 – 200.00. Author's collection.

Brooch combines culturally and color-wise with south-of-the-border wool jacket. Black turtleneck and black pants complete the outfit.

Same brooch worn with gray pine color outfit.

Sterling bird brooch, nearly 6" long. Marked Los Castillo. C. 1945. $400.00 – 500.00. Courtesy of Sandra Samaniego.

Sterling bird brooches, each almost 5½" long. Both unmarked. C. 1940s. $150.00 – 200.00 each. Elena Quinones collection.

Copper bird brooch, marked Victoria and Taxco. C. 1940 – 1945. $150.00 – 200.00. Courtesy of Sandra Samaniego.

Sterling bird motif brooches, all unattributed. Marked Taxco. C. 1940. $100.00 – 200.00 each. Elena Quinones collection.

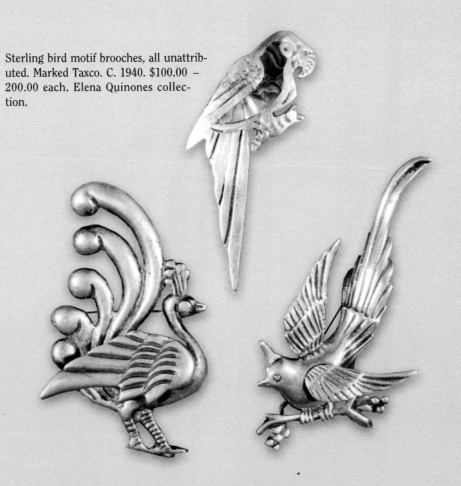

Turquoise, amethyst, and coral brooch. Marked MATL, indicating that the maker was Matilde Poulat. $300.00. Courtesy of Sandra Samaniego.

Brooch of pre-Columbian design with cascabeles (small bells hung in rows along the underside of jewels). Marked Maricela Isidro Garcia. C. 1950. $85.00 – 100.00. Courtesy of Sandra Samaniego.

Sterling and bezel-set stone necklace and earring combination. Marked Los Ballesteros. C. 1941. $250.00 – 350.00 set. Elena Quinones collection.

Kristin wears the fish skeleton necklace/earring set with a black tank, jeans, and black open-collared shirt.

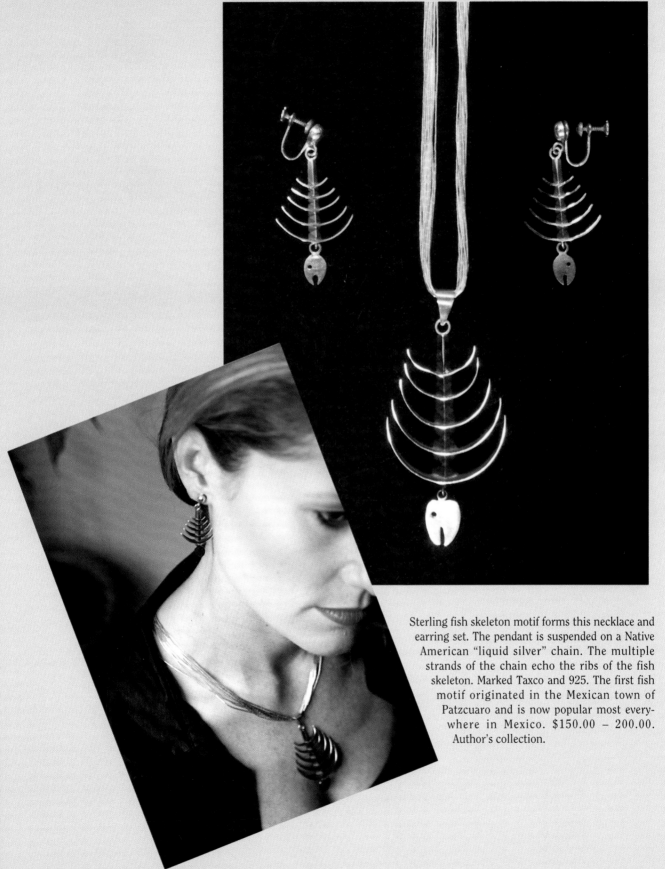

Sterling fish skeleton motif forms this necklace and earring set. The pendant is suspended on a Native American "liquid silver" chain. The multiple strands of the chain echo the ribs of the fish skeleton. Marked Taxco and 925. The first fish motif originated in the Mexican town of Patzcuaro and is now popular most everywhere in Mexico. $150.00 – 200.00. Author's collection.

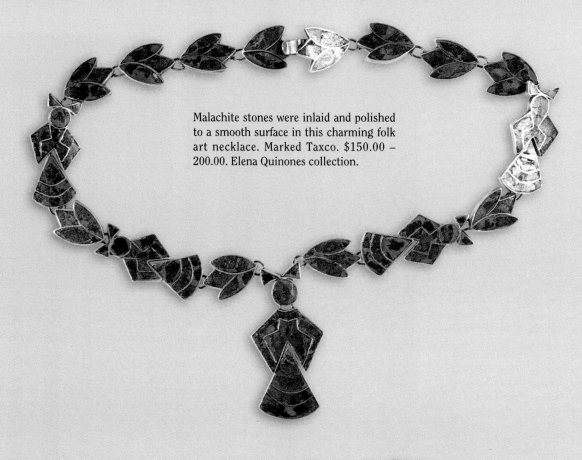

Malachite stones were inlaid and polished to a smooth surface in this charming folk art necklace. Marked Taxco. $150.00 – 200.00. Elena Quinones collection.

Sterling brooch and necklace with similar pre-Columbian motifs, both by Bernice Goodspeed. C. 1945 – 1950. $250.00 – 300.00. Courtesy of Sandra Samaniego.

Whimsical horse motif depicted in this Los Castillo necklace and bracelet. Marked with the maker's name, Taxco, and 925. C. 1950. $750.00 – 1,000.00. Author's collection.

Very old Mexican bracelet, unattributed, and marked Taxco and 980. Note old clasp style. C. 1920 – 1930. $300.00 – 350.00. Author's collection.

his bracelet can
e worn with most anything.

Sterling and aventurine (aventurine quartz is also called "Indian jade") cabochon stone necklace and earring set. C. 1960. Marked Antonio Pineda. $1,200.00 – 1,500.00. Author's collection.

On the left, Sara wears the Los Ballesteros pendant necklace and on the right, Melissa wears the Antonio Pineda necklace and earring set shown above. Both women accent their simple white tops with colorful and eye-catching jewels.

This Los Ballesteros round pendant incorporates several pre-Hispanic symbols from the Aztec calendar stone and a faceted citrine in the center. There has been criticism for miniaturizing the calendar stone because it is actually of monumental size and is covered with intricate symbols which are considered lost when made small for jewelry purposes. But it remains a very popular motif, used in Mexican jewelry for many years. It was even used by William Spratling in pendant form. C. 1940s – 1950s. $200.00 – 300.00. Author's collection.

The pendant can be worn any time of year. Here, it is worn with a fall outfit and on the opposite page, Sarah wears it for summer.

Kristin wears the matching sterling belt and bracelet with a long gray sweater dress and cowboy boots.

Sterling belt and bracelet set is marked Taxco and 925. Unattributed. $300.00 – 350.00 set. Author's collection.

Marcel Boucher sterling brooches, marked Parasina.
C. 1940 – 1945. $150.00 – 250.00 each. Courtesy of
Sandra Samaniego.

William Spratling brooches. C. 1943.
$500.00 – 600.00 each. Courtesy of Sandra
Samaniego.

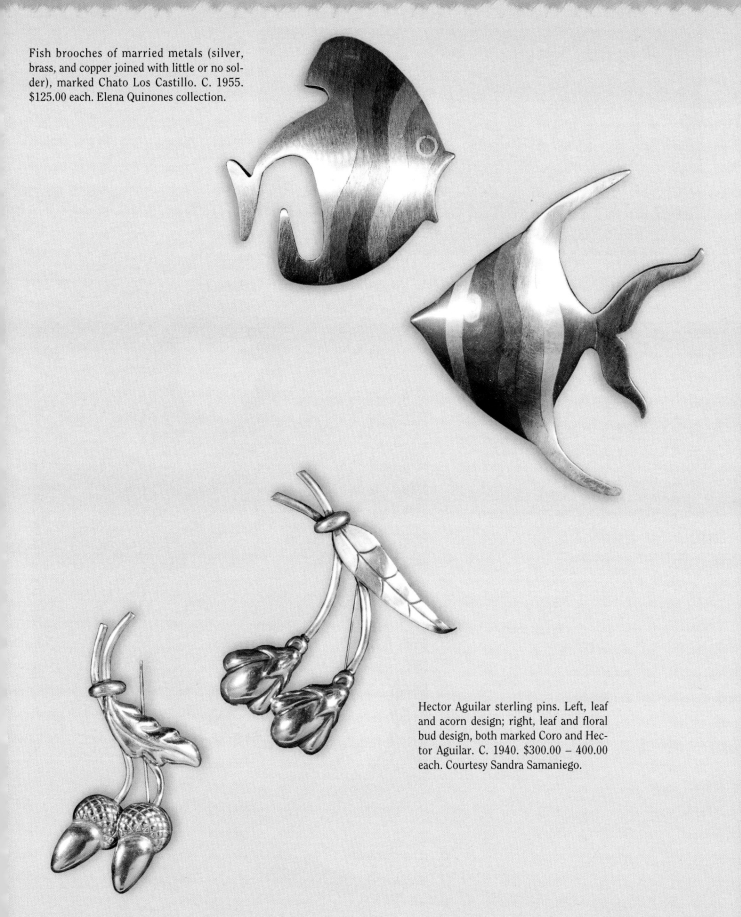

Fish brooches of married metals (silver, brass, and copper joined with little or no solder), marked Chato Los Castillo. C. 1955. $125.00 each. Elena Quinones collection.

Hector Aguilar sterling pins. Left, leaf and acorn design; right, leaf and floral bud design, both marked Coro and Hector Aguilar. C. 1940. $300.00 – 400.00 each. Courtesy Sandra Samaniego.

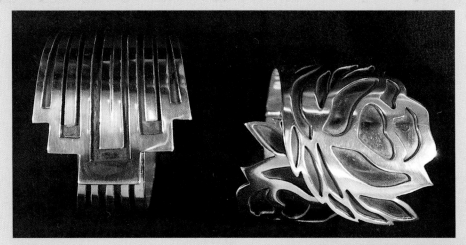

Two sterling bracelets utilizing pattern cut-outs and oxidizing to blacken the resulting recesses. Top of pattern is polished to high patina. These hinged, old bracelets are marked Taxco and 980. $350.00 – 400.00. Author's collection.

Pre-Hispanic Indians — Olmecs, Mayans, and Aztecs — considered the jaguar to be lord of the jungle because of its power, in essence a god. Their art shows human/jaguar combinations such as the jaguar knight and even humanized jaguars. Any kind of animal print, be it jaguar, tiger, leopard, even zebra, is a cultural natural when combined with Mexican jewelry.

Hector Aguilar sterling bracelets, marked HE.
Top: Coro squares bracelet, $400.00 – 500.00;
middle: bird bracelet, $600.00 – 700.00; and
bottom: lyre bracelet, $900.00 – 1,000.00.
Courtesy of Sandra Samaniego.

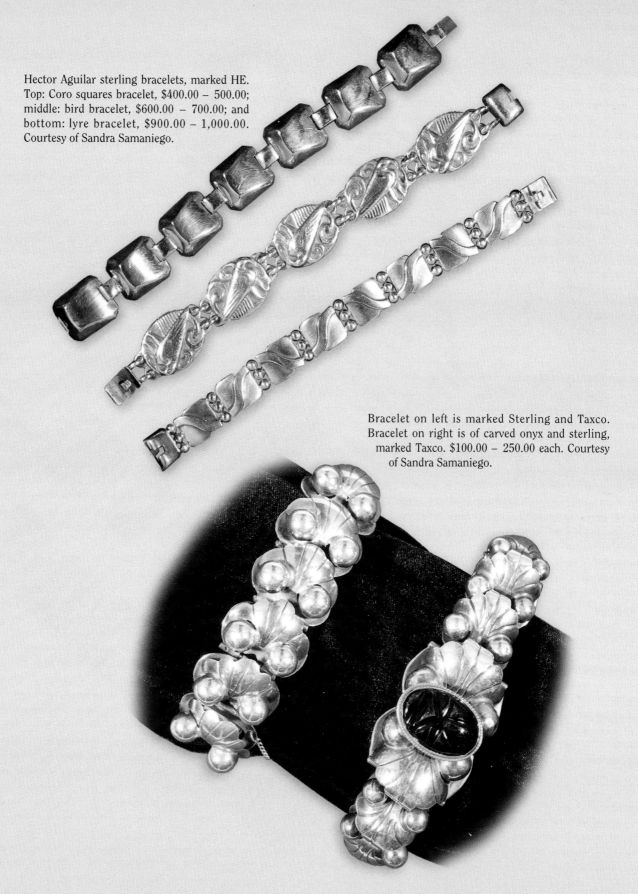

Bracelet on left is marked Sterling and Taxco.
Bracelet on right is of carved onyx and sterling,
marked Taxco. $100.00 – 250.00 each. Courtesy
of Sandra Samaniego.

Sara, Melissa, and Kristin wear abalone (also called concha) shell jewelry with their simple summer outfits.

Each bracelet is composed of a decorative pattern of mother-of-pearl, inlaid into sterling silver. Each design is very different, showing the versatility and creativeness of the designer's imagination. $100.00 – 200.00. Author's collection.

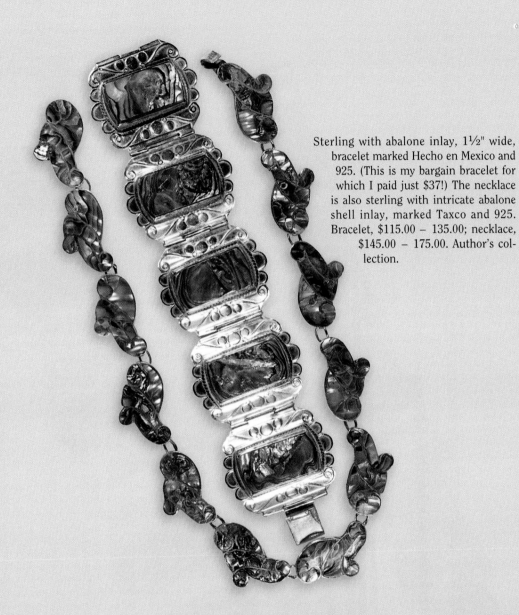

Sterling with abalone inlay, 1½" wide, bracelet marked Hecho en Mexico and 925. (This is my bargain bracelet for which I paid just $37!) The necklace is also sterling with intricate abalone shell inlay, marked Taxco and 925. Bracelet, $115.00 – 135.00; necklace, $145.00 – 175.00. Author's collection.

The butterfly brooch is a handmade masterpiece of inlaid jade and concha shell (chips of stones and shells are set on an adhesive which covers a metal base then polished to a flat surface.) Marked Taxco, CAO, and 925. C. 1930s. $165.00. Abalone shell leaf pin, marked Taxco, CCC, and 925, $75.00 – 85.00. Author's collection.

Abalone and sterling fan and parrot pins, $75.00 – 125.00 each. Concha and tortoise bracelet marked Taxco, $225.00. Elena Quinones collection.

There are so many iridescent colors in concha shell that you could wear most any simple top. This bracelet is especially abundant in blues, greens, and pinks, so that it really sets off a blue cotton T-shirt.

Concha shell inlay hinged bracelet. For the shell inlay, a simple geometric silver design was used to emphasize the pattern of the shell itself. Marked Taxco and Los Ballesteros. $185.00 – 275.00. C. 1950. Author's collection.

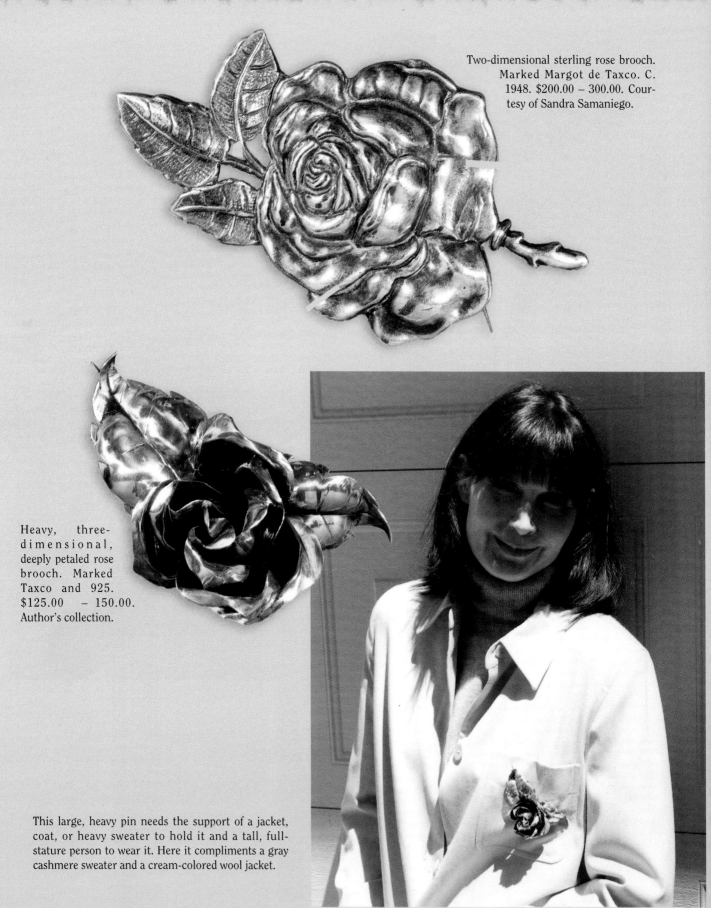

Two-dimensional sterling rose brooch. Marked Margot de Taxco. C. 1948. $200.00 – 300.00. Courtesy of Sandra Samaniego.

Heavy, three-dimensional, deeply petaled rose brooch. Marked Taxco and 925. $125.00 – 150.00. Author's collection.

This large, heavy pin needs the support of a jacket, coat, or heavy sweater to hold it and a tall, full-stature person to wear it. Here it compliments a gray cashmere sweater and a cream-colored wool jacket.

Hector Aguilar sterling and obsidian (a form of natural glass formed from molten lava, which solidified without crystallizing, brittle and very hard to carve and polish) earrings. C. 1940. $200.00 – 300.00. Courtesy of Sandra Samaniego.

Sterling with obsidian pin and earrings. Marked Enrique Ledesma, Taxco, Mexico, and 925. C. 1955. $200.00 – 300.00 set. Courtesy of Sandra Samaniego.

Sterling, hand-made necklace in a very early style. Although it is unmarked, I believe it is a Los Castillo. Sometimes, often, actually, parures are sold separately and since only one piece of the parure may be marked, the identifying stamp may be missing on the remainder of the set. C. 1940. The necklace identification would need to be authenticated to establish a price. Author's collection.

Melissa wears this necklace with black.

The handmade necklace brightens up a busy print but almost disappears in the process.

Karen wears the same necklace, which adds glimmer to a somewhat somber gray outfit.

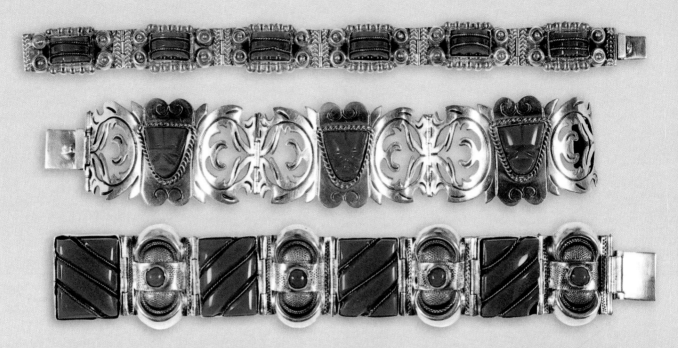

Three green onyx bracelets. Gem quality onyx marble is an opaque calcite found primarily in Baja California, Mexico and is commonly called Mexican onyx or if dyed green, Mexican jade.
C. 1950s. $125.00 – 250.00 each. Author's collection.

Uncarved jade cabochon bracelet, marked Sterling, Mexico, and MR (unknown maker).
C. 1945. $150.00 – 200.00. Courtesy of Sandra Samaniego.

Charm bracelet marked Taxco. C. 1940. Charms represent the quetzal bird, an old coin, fruits, miner with backpack, drum, and several religious symbols. $150.00 – 200.00. Elena Quinones collection.

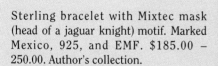

Sterling bracelet with Mixtec mask (head of a jaguar knight) motif. Marked Mexico, 925, and EMF. $185.00 – 250.00. Author's collection.

Mexican and Native American jewelry can often be worn together because of their long-standing historical and cultural associations. Keep styles similar when wearing together. This Mexican silver necklace has blackened recessed areas and the silver Native American bracelet also has a blackened motif. Necklace marked Los Castillo. $350.00 – 450.00. Bracelet is unmarked. $85.00 – 125.00. Author's collection.

Repoussé (shaped with patterns made by hammering or pressing on the reverse side) sterling bracelet, marked Alfredo Villasana. C. 1955. $250.00 – 300.00. Courtesy of Sandra Samaniego.

Sterling bracelet marked CA and Taxco. $200.00 – 300.00. Courtesy of Sandra Samaniego.

This bracelet is worn correctly — so any observer can see the carved face right side up when the arm is extended.

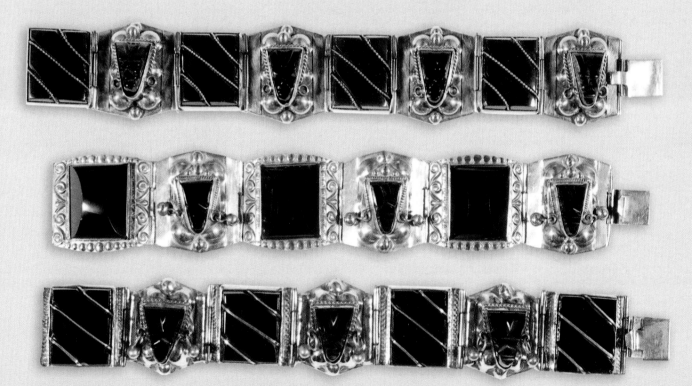

Three carved face and rectangular stone bracelets, showing varying degrees of detail and workmanship. C. 1950. $150.00 – 250.00 each. Author's collection.

If you already have on a major focus of interest, perhaps a leopard belt with large gold buckle, keep any other accessories to a minimum and at the same physical level as the major focus, so that the eye isn't pulled from place to place. Be sure that the accessories are culturally and color compatible. This bracelet is unusual with its gold background color. Marked Taxco and 925. $250.00.

Sterling necklace using repouseé technique. C. 1945.
$150.00 – 250.00. Elena Quinones collection.

Like other vintage clothes which are 60 or 70 years old, this Mexican jacket shows signs of wear. There are several moth holes in the wool, scattered outside the embroidered areas of the fabric. Because of the many colorful scenes in the jacket, you could miss the Mexican jade carved face brooch on the model's left shoulder, which hides a prominent moth hole. This jacket provides a good example of an additional utilitarian attribute of jewelry, especially in regards to vintage clothing. It is useful for camouflaging moth holes, stains, or any missing areas of decorative motifs. At the very least, it can divert attention from a flaw.

Although this particular jacket is not too large, its size could be adjusted if it were. Just gather fabric in the back of the jacket, just above waist level (for a leggy look), with a large brooch.

Mexican jade carved face brooch with ornate sterling headdress and earrings. Marked Taxco and 925. $100.00 – 150.00. Author's collection.

Sterling silver, handmade cross embellished with six hanging crosses. The main cross is stamped Taxco, Sterling, and JCB. Handmade chain. $250.00 – 350.00. Private collection.

The cross is worn here with a simple white cotton top and black imitation leather jeans. The cross makes an inexpensive outfit look rich and adds an interesting focal point.

This handmade necklace is the oldest piece in the author's collection. The main coin, set eagle side up, is dated 1868 and inscribed "Libertad" and "Republica Mexicana." The small coins are dated 1878, 1895, and 1896, and each has a hole in it so that they could be strung together (before being made into this necklace) to prevent them from getting lost. There are horses soldered on the top of the main coin, as well as a quetzal bird, a cock, and some type of bushy-tailed animal hanging from chains from the small coins. The silver content of the coins was mined in Mexico and also minted there. Earlier coins served as standard international currency and were even legal tender in the United States until 1857. $350.00 – 400.00.

The coin necklace is so elaborate that all it really needs is the simplest of backgrounds. In several shades of gray, a solid-color top, pants, and shoes compose the background ensemble.

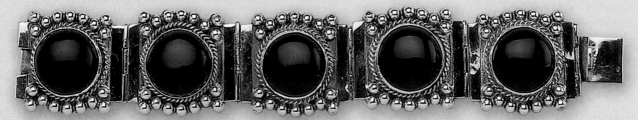

Cabochon onyx stone and sterling bracelet. Marked Taxco and 980. $175.00 – 250.00.

Carved head onyx stone and sterling hinged bracelet. Marked Taxco and Sterling. $150.00 – 250.00.

Three-paneled sterling bracelet with
ball-type design surrounding hinges.
Marked Taxco and 925. $150.00 – 200.00.

Acknowledgments

Thank you to the authors listed in the Bibliography from whom I learned so much. Due to my hospital work schedule, I had no time for personal interviews, travels to distant places, or research of obscure dissertations. I appreciate the knowledge that you imparted.

Kudos to my dear friend Bill Nader for his invaluable historical perspective, for his discerning eye for quality and dependability, and for the beautiful jewelry that he has introduced into my life. I am profoundly grateful.

Gratitude to Sandra Samaniego, Elena Quinones, and Joe Goure of Betty's House of Turquoise for sharing their personal collections with me. Thank you also to the private collectors who trusted me with their treasures but wish to remain anonymous. These kindred spirits inspired me and joined in my enthusiasm for the project.

Much appreciation to the folks at Motophoto who responded to my endless requests with a smile and superior results.

I'd like to and express thanks and recognition to our beautiful models Jeannie Cervantes, Kristin MacDonell, Melissa Reed, and Sara Vance. They unstintingly gave time from their busy schedules and contributed many creative ideas for the fashion photographs.

Thank you to Janine Mapurunga Connolly, a most professional, fun, and innovative artist whose eye for beauty in winter twigs, converging lines in a fence or in a mirrored image led to fabulous indoor and outdoor photos, and to Chris Vance and Justin Lewis, our wonderful photographers who untiringly gave their best to produce the fashion images.

A special award to my beloved daughter Kristin for her willingness to be a "model extraordinaire," for driving three hundred miles round-trip to cook for us when I injured my back, and for being the best, most caring and supportive daughter there ever could be.

But most of all thank you to my beloved husband George who has uncomplainingly critiqued countless rewrites, endured many canned soup "dinners," and accepted utter chaos in our home as I prepared this book. With his commitment to the book, as to every aspect of our lives, he has made all things possible.

About the Author

I have worked for twenty-five years as a nuclear medicine technologist. For these years my milieu has been sickness, pain, death, and suffering. As a single mother, I appreciated every employed day; every emergency callback (well, maybe not every one, especially those which happened in the middle of the night); and every overtime hour because it offered a good living while providing a needed service. But when off-duty, my interests could blossom and my interest for almost ten years has been jewelry. I have enjoyed every carefree, fun-filled minute that I spent foraging for fabulous jewels. I discovered jewelry about which I had never known: well-crafted, well-designed treasures.

My fascination with jewelry began at a garage sale. The owner had amassed quite a large collection, part of which was now up for sale to raise money to send her son to medical school. Included was a type of jewelry unfamiliar to me called Bakelite. I began to search everywhere for it but became frustrated and angry, naively buying plastics falsely advertised as Bakelite. The price of this hot collectible was way beyond what I wanted to spend. As a result of my searches, I started to notice other types of jewelry. I learned to look for marks or stamps on jewels which bore a company logo. This mark gave assurance that the item was authentic, that someone or some company took enough pride in their product to stamp their name on it. I started reading everything I could about jewelry, attending gem shows and antique shops, and comparing prices to find quality pieces.

Of course, I had to talk about my newfound passion at work. But I noticed that when I described antique and collectible jewelry to co-workers, they inevitably associated it with "what my grandmother used to wear." It was perceived as being outdated, cobwebbed whims which were fancied only by odd collectors. My enthusiasm was greeted by wan smiles accompanied by my friends' equivalent of "how nice" remarks. Yet when I later wore the jewels, these same women commented: "You have such beautiful jewelry."; "I'm going on my vacation to Mexico and I want to find one exactly like it"; or "You know it's my birthday coming up. . ." This jewelry is not something "old grandma" at all. It is young (glittering costume), playful (figural copper), and luxe (handmade Native American and Mexican) looking. It is supremely wearable, will gild the lily, and is an investment to boot!

One day, the combining of vocation and avocation briefly occurred when my supervisor at the hospital walked in with a bag full of her old, unwanted jewelry for a co-worker's young daughter. As the female employees sifted through the contents, our supervisor sighed and said, "Behind every piece, there's a story." This anecdote exemplifies another reason why I became smitten with antique jewelry. It is not only an investment and a piece of art, but also a tangible embodiment of emotions and experiences. Each piece is bought to complement an outfit, wear to a special event, celebrate a milestone, remember a memorable trip or perhaps a loved one.

In the case of handmade jewelry, undoubtedly there were also compelling circumstances involved in its creation. These human stories add richness and meaning to the ownership of antique hand-wrought and unique jewelry.

My husband and I reside in Sacramento, California, and are regular patrons of the local theaters and opera houses. We also enjoy gardening and traveling.

Bibliography

Arritt, Susan and Marc Simmons. "The Allure of Turquoise." *New Mexico Magazine,* 1995.

Baker, Lillian. *Fifty Years of Collectible Fashion Jewelry.* Collector Books, 1986.

Ball, Joanne. *Costume Jewelers.* Schiffer, 1990.

Bassman, Theda and Michael. *Zuni Jewelry.* Schiffer Publishing, 1992.

Burkholz, Matthew and Linda Kaplan. *Copper Art Jewelry, A Different Luster.* Schiffer, 1992.

Burland, Cottie and Forman. *The Aztecs, Gods and Fate in Ancient Mexico.* Galahad Books, 1980.

Chang, Jung. *Wild Swans.* Anchor Books, 1991.

Coe, Michael D. *The Art of the Maya Scribe.* Harry N. Abrams, Inc., 1998.

Davis, Mary L. and Greta Pack. *Mexican Jewelry.* University of Texas Press, 1963.

Editors Time-Life Books. *Aztecs: Reign of Blood and Splendor.* Time-Life Books, 1992.

Fales, Martha Gandy. *Jewelry in America.* Antique Collectors Club Ltd., 1995.

Hackney, Ki and Diana Edkins. *People and Pearls, the Magic Endures.* Harper Collins Publishers, 2000.

Jacka, Lois Essary. *Navajo Jewelry.* Northland Publishing, 1995.

Jargstorf, Sibylle. *Glass in Jewelry.* Schiffer Publishing, 1991.

Jennings, Kate. *Remington and Russell and the Art of the American West.* Brompton Books Corp, 1993.

Joyce, Kristin and Shellei Addison. *Pearls, Ornament and Obsession.* Simon and Schuster, 1993.

Katz-Schwartz, Judith. *Collector's Compass.* Martingale and Co., 2000.

Kelly, Lyngerda and Nancy Schiffer. *Costume Jewelry, The Great Pretenders.* Schiffer Books, 1996.

Massie, Robert. *Nicholas and Alexandra.* Ballantine Publishing Group, 1967.

McNab, Nan. *Body Bizarre Body Beautiful.* Simon and Schuster, 1999.

Miller, Harrice. *Official Identification and Price Guide to Costume Jewelry.* Avon Books, 1990.

Miller, Mary Ellen. *Maya Art and Architecture.* Thames and Judson Ltd., London, 1999.

Morrill, Penny and Carole Berk. *Mexican Silver, 20th Century Handwrought Jewelry and Metalwork.* Schiffer, 1994.

Morrill, Penny. *Silver Masters of Mexico.* Schiffer Publishing, 1996.

National Geographic, Vol. 121, No. 4. April, 1962: Vol. 121, No. 5. May, 1962: Vol. 131, No. 3. March 1967; Vol. 200, No. 1. July 2001.

Parkinson, Cornelia. *Gem Magic.* Ballantine Books, 1988.

Prescott, William. *The Conquest of Mexico.* The Modern Library, 1936.

Reader's Digest. *Mysteries of the Ancient Americas.* The Reader's Digest Association, Inc, 1986.

Reddish, Paul. *Spirits of the Jaguar.* BBC Books, 1996.

Rezazadeh, Fred. *Costume Jewelry, A Practical Handbook and Value Guide.* Collector Books, 1998.

Russell, Lynn. *Rainbow of Rhinestone Jewelry.* Schiffer, 1996.

San Francisco Chronicle. "Politics of the ancient Maya rested on the written word." July 21, 2001.

Schiffer, Nancy. *Rhinestones!.* Schiffer, 1993.

Schiffer, Nancy. *Silver Jewelry Treasures.* Schiffer, 1996.

Simonds, Cherri. *Collectible Costume Jewelry, Identification and Values.* Collector Books, 1997.

Smith, Bradley. *Mexico, A History in Art.* Doubleday and Company, Inc., 1968.

Smithsonian Magazine. August 1999, January 2000, March 2000, and July 2001.

Sofianides, Anna and George Harlow. *Gems and Crystals from the American Museum of Natural History.* Simon and Schuster, 1990.

Thompson, Eric. *Mexico Before Cortez.* Charles Scribner's Sons, 1937.

Time Magazine. June 7, 1999.

Tolkien, Tracy and Henrietta Wilkinson. *A Collector's Guide to Costume Jewelry. Key styles and how to recognize them.* Firefly Books, 1997.

Turnbaugh, William and Sarah. *Indian Jewelry of the American Southwest.* Schiffer Publishing, 1996.

Vaillant, George. *Aztecs of Mexico.* Doubleday and Company, Inc., 1962.

Wilson, Mab. *Gems.* The Viking Press, Inc., 1967.

Index

ML

5/
02